Our Storm

By:

Jeremy & Tiffany Pollard

bumpsbruisesandgrace.com
tiffanypollard1@gmail.com

About Jeremy & Tiffany:

Jeremy and Tiffany met their first week of college and were married 3 years later. They are blessed with a busy home made up of four boys and one girl. Currently they live in Mebane, NC, where Jeremy is the Campus Pastor at the Summit Church's Alamance Campus. Jeremy enjoys playing golf on the occasional free weekend. Tiffany is a stay at home Mom and enjoys reading and writing.

Table of Contents

Acknowledgements

"But now, this is what the Lord says-he who created you, O Jacob, he who formed you, O Israel; 'Fear not, for I have redeemed you; I have summoned you by name, you are mine. When you pass through the waters, I will be with you; and when you pass through the rivers, they will not sweep over you. When you walk through the fire, you will not be burned; the flames will not set you ablaze'."
-Isaiah 43:1,2

Within the pages that follow lies our story. Everyone has a story, and this one is ours. Jeremy and I have termed it "Our Storm." Just as the winds pick up and the clouds gather without notice, sometimes life does the same. And just as quickly as these storms pass, our lives move on. The ramifications, however, are often felt forever.

In our case, we have been amazed by the storm God sent into our lives. Yes, we see this as His doing. He has been and will always be in control. Our families' lives were shaken on August 27 but not our faith. We seek to share what God has done in praise to Him.

Neither Jeremy nor I claim to be writers. This rough portrayal of our journey has been written for personal reasons. There are so many little details we want to remember. God did too many miracles for us to forget. We want Stephen to have something to look back at in the years to come. When we are too old to remember it all, may he read these pages and be reminded of what God did in our lives. May Stephen remember that God has a purpose for his life.

We have also written for our families. They lived this with us. May they read and realize how God used them. May they cherish the good times and the blessings of another day.

In an attempt to remember as much as possible, we are still confident things have been left out; not purposefully but because our limited minds could never hold it all. We have written from our perspective. We have recorded what we remember. Others who walked this road with us may be able to add more details. Jeremy and I have written as we saw things; as we lived our storm.

When God works, it should be shared. We can't keep these miracles a secret. God was so real to us; so close. May those who read see His perfect hand. We pray others' (and our own as we re-walk this road) faith be strengthened. God has been so good! Let us strive to know Him better.

It has been our privilege to write each word of our story. We are amazed that God allowed us to go through this storm; that He chose us to reveal Himself so clearly. Admittedly it has also been hard as Jeremy and I have re-lived different moments and emotions we have felt. We have taken breaks in the writing process as the pain was too hard to bear. Healing, however, has also taken place with the press of each key. We know it was His will that we write. Thank You God for this opportunity.

This book is dedicated to our family and friends. Thank you for sacrificing your lives for us. Thank you for putting everything else on hold. We could not have made it through without each of you. You did things for us beyond the world's conception of love. We have learned from your example. May we be better friends and parents as a result. God chose you as He did us. Our families mean more to us than could be expressed.

We also dedicate this book to our family in Christ. The prayers sent up around the world made all the difference. Thank you for your love and support. Thank you, Union Grove, for walking through this with us. Students and leaders at the GROVE, you are more precious to us than you will ever comprehend. We are proud of you.

To the staff and families of the Summit Church, thank you for welcoming us into your family only a year after our Storm. We were still broken and floundering. But God led us here, and you have loved us well. Your listening ears helped us heal. We cannot imagine serving with a greater group of friends.

We dedicate this to the child waiting for us in Heaven. Each day we long to see your beautiful face. You paid a greater price than anyone else; yet you are already receiving the greatest reward. We will forever hold you in our hearts and eventually in our arms. To the child now growing inside my womb, we also dedicate this book to you. Your family already loves you so deeply. Precious, Caleb, may you feel the love of God as soon as you enter this world. We are waiting!

This book is also dedicated to Stephen. We love you so much, son. Each day is a gift to be treasured. God could have taken you on August 27. In His plan He chose to leave you on this earth. The Father has a special plan for your life. He is asking for willingness, not perfection. May your

Daddy and Mommy never let you forget that you are here for a purpose. We live with such responsibility. We are sorry that you had to suffer. Our hearts broke with each tear; with each cry that we were unable to console. We knew, though, and we know each day, that God is holding you. He loves you even more than we do. Thank you for being our son. It is our joy to love you!

Lastly, we dedicate this book to our Father. Words are too futile to explain our thankfulness. God has proven our Shelter and our Shepherd. He has worked things out the way only He could. We could see His hand even when we couldn't understand what He was doing. Thank You, Lord. Your plans are always perfect. We know You never make mistakes. Thank You for giving our family another day to share together. Thank You for giving us life. Some days we yearn to be with You. We imagine the perfect joy we could be experiencing right now. But we know You left us here for a purpose. Life is much sweeter now. May we serve

You wholeheartedly and live our lives in such a way that others see You. Our family has traveled through and came out of a storm. We are better for it. Thank You for August 27. Thank You for the heartache. Thank You for the joy. "Our Storm" is for Your glory!

1

Monday, August 27

"I took you from the ends of the earth, from its farthest

corners I called you. I said, 'You are my servant'; I have

chosen you and have not rejected you. So do not fear, for I

am with you; do not be dismayed, for I am your God. I will

strengthen you and help you; I will uphold you with my

righteous right hand."

-Isaiah 41:9,10

Months back I had read somewhere that Psalm

118:24 was a great verse to quote each morning with your

child. So, in an attempt to be "great parents," our family

began quoting Psalm 118:24 each morning at breakfast.

"This is the day that the Lord has made; we will rejoice and

be glad in it." We'd read a Proverb, Jeremy and I would

tag-team quoting the verse, and we'd conclude things with

prayer. It may not have meant much to our 16-month old,

Stephen, but it was an important part of what we believed.

This Monday, August 27, began the same as any other day. I'd gotten up before my family, took a brisk prayer walk through the neighborhood, spent some quiet time in God's Word, and looked over my plans for the day. Feeling more prepared, I headed to the bathroom to get "physically ready." Jeremy was already up and getting dressed for work. After a good morning, quick kiss, and short conversation, the sounds of a waking baby came through the monitor. The day, whether we were ready or not, had officially started.

Our son, Stephen Andrew, was a large part of who we were. He's who gave us the names Daddy and Mommy. He's who made us a family. The 3 years we spent married without children were amazing, but we'd never dream of going back. Stephen's smile had changed our life. The flash of his beating heart at 6 weeks in my womb engrained in our hearts what God was doing. And after all the books and advice, we still weren't prepared for the flood of emotions we'd felt the day he was born.

"Do not boast about tomorrow, for you do not know what a day may bring forth." Jeremy read the first verse of Proverbs 27 aloud as I attempted to keep Stephen attentive in preparation for the next 26. We followed this up with Psalm 118:24, prayer, and an enthusiastic AMEN. Stephen and I finished breakfast, and Jeremy left for work. From the kitchen window Stephen waved "bye-bye" as his Daddy (and favorite playmate) drove out of sight. In a few hours, Jeremy would be returning home for lunch and a special family outing we had planned.

Most of our morning was spent in Stephen's playroom. From books to balls, what brought Stephen joy brought the same to me and Jeremy. How refreshing it is to see things through your child's eyes! During moments when he was preoccupied, I found myself busily organizing drawers and straightening the closet. It was almost like I was cleaning and preparing our home for someone else to live in. I chalked it up to nesting. Jeremy and I had found out on Friday that we were expecting our second child. We had shared the news with both his parents and mine over the weekend. We were thrilled and had calculated that this child and Stephen would be about 2 years apart-*our plan* from the start. Everything seemed perfect.

Around 11:00 Stephen ran to the door after hearing the garage open. Jeremy was home just in time for us to leave. One of my longtime favorite groups was performing a free concert at the mall, and we had planned on going for weeks. I was supposed to start back to work today but had moved all of my students to Tuesday. It seemed important for us to spend this day as a family. While putting Stephen in the car, Jeremy noticed that Stephen's car seat was not securely strapped in. We had recently moved it from one vehicle to the other and forgotten to secure it properly. In a rush, I reminded myself to do it when we returned home.

We arrived at the mall about 30 minutes before the concert began. Stephen had fallen asleep on the way, so Jeremy carefully transferred him to his stroller. After grabbing lunch, we found just the right spot to watch the concert. It was better than I anticipated. The concert included songs from some of the group's older albums and from their new CD. About midway through, Stephen woke up. Jeremy and I passed him back and forth in order to keep him occupied. During one of their new songs "How You Live," I stood close to Jeremy as he held Stephen. The words "Kiss all your children, dance with your wife, tell your husband you love him, every night…" were a beautiful reminder of how deeply God had blessed our family. I could barely hold back the tears. With a Godly husband, healthy son, and precious baby on the way, I couldn't imagine life being any sweeter.

After the concert, we strolled to the toddler area of the mall. Jeremy and I sat and smiled as Stephen ran from oversized grapes to the banana slide. He had always been such a happy baby. As he had moved from one childhood stage to another, we claimed each as our favorite. This one was no different. We always felt that God had something special in store for our son. Our prayer was "God use him *now*, and use him later." We wanted to see God's hand on his life, not when he was our age, but now, even as a 16-month old. In several hours, our prayer would begin to be answered.

When we got home, Jeremy returned to work, and I put Stephen down for his afternoon nap. During the short time he slept, I tightened the car seat and cleaned the house a little more. Stephen woke up unusually cranky and wanted nothing but for me to hold him. After awhile, he seemed somewhat better, while I began feeling very tired. I sat on our back porch and watched Stephen play in his adjoining playroom. Jeremy's arrival was much appreciated, and he could tell by my face and tears that I needed a break. He had always been great at reading me. I laid on the couch and watched Jeremy and Stephen roughhouse on the floor. There are certain things that a Daddy does best.

Jeremy and Stephen laughed and played until it was time for supper. We ate and got ready for church. We were having revival until Wednesday, and I was excited to go. Both Jeremy and I felt a deep conviction that God was going to do something great at our church. We had been praying for weeks. I grabbed Stephen's diaper bag, and we headed to the car. Union Grove was only 5 minutes away. We'd be there soon.

*Pulling out of our garage was just like every other time. We had purchased a brand new car about 2 months earlier. I (Jeremy) can still remember the new car smell. Our route that night was not unusual. It was actually very familiar to me, since I had driven it every day for the last couple years. When we built the house, we did so knowing we would be close to our ministry. It was just a short 3 ½ mile trip to the church that night for revival.

Everything was as normal as any other trip. Stephen was in his car seat in the back enjoying the music playing on the radio. He had recently learned to raise his hands up and down to up-tempo music. Tiff was doing the usual on the way to church; finishing her makeup or looking at her hair. I was eagerly waiting to see what God was going to do at revival that night. We had actually left a little early for me to be in a prayer room prior to that night's service. At about 6:45 that evening we were about a mile away from our house, headed down a steep hill on a nearby highway.

The car in front of ours swerved slightly to miss an oncoming vehicle. That oncoming vehicle was an SUV that had crossed into our lane. The moment of seeing the vehicle in our lane to the moment of impact seemed shorter than a second. The time was only long enough for me to apply the brakes, to begin swerving to the right, and to let out two words, "HOLD ON." The results of the impact were typical of a head-on collision involving an SUV and a small sedan. As one can imagine, our small 4-door sedan easily took the brunt of the collision. With the estimated speed of both vehicles clocking in at around 50 mph, there wasn't much left of the front end of our new, little car.

In the minutes to follow, everything is strangely still very familiar to me. I can remember the exact moment that the ambulances, fire trucks, and highway patrolmen arrived. The extent of our injuries was unclear then, but what was very clear was that Tiff's airbag had not deployed. As an obvious result of that, Tiff's forehead had shattered the windshield at impact, and she was in and out of consciousness. Concerning my immediate injuries, I felt extreme pain in both of my legs. The dashboard crunched on my legs made it impossible for me to even move. Adrenaline, however, had taken over. When I was first able to turn and assess Stephen, I could clearly tell that he was not breathing and almost lifeless. That's when I knew that our son, most importantly, needed immediate medical attention.

Before all the great emergency personnel came, *our* heroes came in the form of a few innocent bystanders. First of all, a young man, about our age stopped on the scene to offer his lending hand. I remember him first checking with me and Tiff to find out if we were okay. It was at this time that I told him about Stephen in the back. Because there was no damage to Stephen's side of the car, our first hero, David, was able to easily get Stephen out of his car seat and take him to the side of the road. During this time, he was still unconscious. That's when hero number 2 came into our lives.

Another family traveling down the road at the time of the wreck also stopped to offer their help. The husband got into the backseat of the car to talk to us and try to keep us calm. His face is one of the few that Tiff remembers. His wife, a nurse in training, took Stephen and began CPR on him immediately. It wasn't very long until I heard Stephen crying on the side of the road, which was a welcome relief.

By this time the emergency crew was arriving. They began to open both of the doors and, using the Jaws of Life, to relieve the pressure of the car that had collapsed on me and Tiff. Once we were both out of the vehicles, we were put on stretchers and placed in 2 different ambulances. They transported us to a local hospital about 10 miles away. Our day that had begun so normally was now going to end in serious, life-changing procedures. Our family had entered a storm.

*Jeremy wrote parts of this chapter himself as his memory of the wreck is clearer.

2

Tuesday, August 28-Saturday, September 1

"My flesh and my heart may fail, but God is the strength of my heart and my portion forever."

-Psalm 73:26

Everything that occurred over the next 24 hours is a jumble for both me (Tiffany) and Jeremy. We both vaguely remember the trip to the hospital. The short route seemed like an eternity to both of us. I remember lying in a small room with doctors and nurses all around. I can vividly see my Dad and Mom as they first visited me in the emergency room. Their calmness comforted me during a time of total confusion. I remember telling a nurse I was pregnant prior to entering an "MRI tunnel," and her covering my belly to protect it. These limited memories are all God left me with until the day after the wreck.

Sometime Tuesday I began to wake up and understand the full severity of what had happened. Jeremy lay one bed away from me in the hospital's Trauma Intensive Care Unit. He, however, was still asleep. Many people, both friends and family, came in to see us. I only remember some of them. After awhile I began to understand that there were visiting hours, and I would watch the clock as best I could. Once the lights were cut on, I knew it would not be long until I saw my family. They would stay with me until a nurse asked them to leave. To this day, I cannot fathom the grace God must have given them to endure the pain of seeing both me and Jeremy in this condition.

Our nurses these first couple of days gave us only a taste of how precious men and women in this field are. I remember one of my ICU nurses asking me if there was anything I would like for her to tell Jeremy. I told her to tell him that I loved him but NOT to kiss him! When the patient lying between me and Jeremy would set off his alarms, the nurses would reassure me that it was not Jeremy. Many of them would come in and talk to me with tears in their eyes. I could tell that they truly cared. The weeks ahead would confirm this.

Being careful to protect me, my family had told me only the surface details our injuries. I knew, however, that things were serious for both me and Jeremy. What gave me encouragement, though, was that Stephen had come through the accident with only a few scratches. He was staying in a regular room and would soon be going home. I had made the decision to let him stay with Joe and Judy, a dear couple in our church, until Jeremy and I could join him. This comfort diminished on the white coat tails of a young neurosurgeon.

On Wednesday, surrounded by both my parents and Jeremy's, I learned that Stephen now lay in the Pediatric Intensive Care Unit. After the insistence of Jeremy's oldest brother, David, further tests had been done. God had put David in Stephen's room at the right time. These tests revealed that Stephen had a collapsed lung, and a breathing tube had been inserted. The force of the impact had also torn the ligaments in his neck that connected his skull to his spinal cord. On Friday our son would be facing a complicated 4 to 5 hour surgery.

During this first of many meetings with doctors, I never heard the words, "It will be okay." The point of our ICU meeting that particular day was simply to inform me of what was happening. As Stephen's mother, I had to know. My Dad signed the papers for us since neither Jeremy nor I were able. The situation was extreme. Our whole family now lay in the middle of a severe and still brewing storm.

On Thursday I was told I would be having another surgery. At this time, I still did not understand the surgeries that both Jeremy and I had already undergone. This time the doctors were going to be repairing both my right ankle and my right wrist. I was worried about being sedated, but my nurses reassured me that it would be okay. As they rolled me into the operating room, I remember saying, "Let's do it."

The surgery went well, and I was moved from ICU to Acute Care later that night. I remember when they pushed me by Jeremy's bed. All I could say was, "I love you." On the way to my new room, I heard our teenagers' cry as they caught their first glimpse of me since the wreck. I wondered who was there for them. Jeremy and I were usually the ones who did the comforting. That night in Acute Care was long and uncomfortable. Stephen's upcoming surgery lay heavy on my mind.

After much discussion, I was moved Friday to a regular room on the 11th floor. There were no set visiting hours, and my family stayed with me constantly. Numerous friends and extended family came by with encouraging words. Later that same day we found out that Stephen's surgery had been postponed. He was running a fever. The procedure had been rescheduled for Wednesday; 5 whole days away. The PICU would be Stephen's home for the next week. The ICU would be Jeremy's. And Room 11-03 would be mine. Each member of our family lay on different floors of the hospital. We were apart yet needing each other more than ever.

Saturday morning was spent adjusting to life in my new room. Many different doctors and nurses came in and out. It seemed that every time I moved something different hurt. The injuries that both Jeremy and I had suffered were more real than ever. I began to understand the road that lay ahead. Things began to sink in.

During the surgery I had undergone just 2 days earlier, a plate and screws had been inserted into both my wrist and ankle. The night of the wreck I had another surgery. Part of this surgery included the placement of a rod in my upper left leg. It ran from my hip to my knee. It would serve as my femur bone, which had been broken.

The other part of the surgery had been exploratory. I had been bleeding internally, and the doctors were not sure why. The cause ended up being a torn lower bowel which was repaired. I had also broken my sternum and 3 ribs. My knee had been gashed, along with my upper forehead. In total, I had 42 staples and numerous stitches.

Jeremy also had undergone surgery the night of the accident. He had broken both of his femurs and a rod had been inserted in each leg. These rods, like mine, ran from his hip to his knee. He had also broken his left ankle, left wrist, and crushed his right heel. Both the wrist and heel would require future surgeries. Jeremy, however, still lay in ICU. He had never woken up after the Monday night surgery. I was very confused. My last working memories of Jeremy had been in our crumpled car. He was so alert and calm at the accident scene. I knew he had been seriously hurt, but I could not understand why he was still lying unconscious in ICU. That night we would learn.

So many people wanted to come and visit me. With Jeremy and Stephen both sedated, I was the only one who could communicate. Even then, my racing mind often struggled to find words and make sense of things. I only remember a handful of the many people who came in. The outreach of concern and compassion was mind-boggling. Pastors both familiar and unfamiliar prayed with me. Friends from our past visited my room with tears in their eyes. Toward the end of the day, however, my body said no more. Others' concern was greatly appreciated, but I needed rest, both physically and mentally. With the help of our church and the nursing staff, we began to limit the number of visitors. It hurt me to do this, especially with our teens, but I knew it was a must. I had to rest and heal.

Saturday night I met Jeremy's primary doctor. I had seen a lot of different doctors but never this one. He unexpectedly came into my room, and I immediately knew that he held important news...Jeremy's lungs had been badly damaged in the wreck. He, like Stephen, was breathing with the help of a ventilator. After surgery, Jeremy had never woke up. His body, in fact, had begun to shut down. All week, his condition had worsened. The doctors were boggled but optimistic. Their best guess was that Jeremy was dealing with a rare syndrome called Fat Embolism. There is no known cure for this disorder. We would have to wait it out. Jeremy could wake up in a couple hours, several months, or never. This limited amount of information was all I was given and really all I could handle that night. I would find out more details about the seriousness of Jeremy's condition in the future.

Once the doctor left my room, the rest of the night became a whirlwind. Jeremy's 2 older brothers, David and Chad, were the next to come in and see me. They sat beside my bed in tears. At the same time that I was speaking to Jeremy's doctor, his family had been meeting with another doctor. This doctor, however, had given them a more negative report. Yes, they knew about the Fat Embolism Syndrome, but they had been told that Jeremy's condition would most likely prove fatal. As they understood it, Jeremy would probably never wake up. I cannot begin to explain the pain I saw in their faces that night. I also cannot begin to explain the peace God gave me. Regardless of which doctor's report was correct, we knew the ultimate Healer.

My family would not have left me alone during this uncertain time, but for some reason I felt that only God and I were in that hospital room. He was closer than even I understood. Could it be that both my husband and son were to be taken from me? Was this His plan from the beginning? Many questions filled my mind, but one verse overshadowed every doubt. "The Lord gave and the Lord has taken away; may the name of the Lord be praised." (Job 1:21). My faith was much weaker than Job's, but I served the same God. His will, no matter how difficult and confusing, was always perfect. He had a plan for our family. He would give us grace to face it. Whatever our Father held in store for the future would be best. He alone knew what tomorrow held. For tonight, we would rest in His arms.

3

Sunday, September 2-Tuesday, September 4

"Cast all your anxiety on him because he cares for you.

And the God of all grace who called you to his eternal

glory in Christ, after you have suffered a little while, will

himself restore you and make you strong, firm and

steadfast."

-I Peter 5:7,10

Sunday, 6 days after the wreck, came and went with

little change. We would realize in the future how difficult

this first day of the week would be for us. Both Jeremy and

I taught Sunday school, and we greatly desired to be

serving our teens. Adjustments would have to be made for

everyone. Our church was already doing a great job of this.

That Sunday's bulletin held important information for us

and a willing church family. Five different committees

were being established, including transportation, food,

home help, cleaning, and yard work. These committees

would be our literal lifeline for the next 4 months of life. What a blessing it is to have a caring church family who understands all Jesus gave up for us and willingly gives up their lives for others.

Our Pastor and his wife, Kim, came over on Monday. There were things that still had to be done. I went over our checkbook with Kim and helped her make a menu for the food committee. Most importantly, Pastor and I discussed Jeremy's goals for our first student meeting, which was planned for this Wednesday. It was hard to imagine things going on without us, but I knew God would work it out. Pastor wanted things done exactly as Jeremy had planned. I shared with him our heart.

Jeremy and I had been organizing this first student night for many weeks now. For the first year ever, we had decided to move our meetings from the fellowship hall to the gym. We knew it would be a difficult transition, especially with the set-up and tear-down. But we also knew we had grown too big for the room we presently met in. If God was going to do the great things we felt sure of, we were going to have to do our part. It was a step of faith for everyone. Our leaders and students' parents had been prepped, and everyone was excited. We dreamed of ministering to 100 teens this year and seeing numerous salvations. How much greater God's plans are than the ones we could ever make!

My Mom and Aunt Brenda had begun the task of decorating my room a few days earlier. The wall was covered with cards and pictures of Jeremy and Stephen. Someone had enlarged the last family picture that had been taken of us. We were standing on a Florida beach with the ocean behind us. All 3 of us were partially wet and sandy. This picture hung in both my room and Jeremy's in ICU. I would look at it often and wonder who those people were. Things were so different. Only by God's grace would we ever get through this. I prayed we would one day be a family again.

Being September, our school was in the middle of the fall sports seasons. Jeremy was the assistant varsity soccer coach to his brother David. The team had red wristbands sewn with our initials, JTS, and the date of the wreck. They wore these each game day in honor of us. Both mine and Jeremy's wristbands hung on the wall.

During the late hours of the nights when sleep wouldn't come, God began reminding me of the things He had been teaching me weeks before the wreck. I had just finished reading Elizabeth George's **A Woman After God's Own Heart**. Through this book God had shown me the importance of priorities. My focus had become God first, then Jeremy, Stephen, and other responsibilities. Now was not the time to lose this focus. God had been teaching me about priorities for *"such a time as this."* As difficult as it may be, my family should still be a priority. It was part of

God's beautiful calling on my life as a wife and Mom. I would start by visiting Jeremy and Stephen for a short time each day.

To get a body as weak as mine in a regular wheelchair proved impossible. Here is where I am convinced God gave me the best nurses in the world. Understanding my desire to see my family, one of these willing servants found a bed-wheelchair combo in a closet. It was covered with dust and obviously unused. Each new nurse who came on duty had to learn how to maneuver it. Two or three people would slide me from my bed to this "pink Cadillac." They would then slowly lift the back of it up to put me in a seated position. Once strapped in, someone would roll me from Jeremy's ICU room to Stephen's. The glances I felt from those I passed mattered none. My heart knew what was important. These visits were a small way of keeping our family together.

Stephen's PICU room was average size. A large window spanned the back wall. I can still vividly see him lying in the little iron bed that had become his home. Small stuffed animals and toys covered the end of the crib. Tubes ran in various directions, while monitors surrounded him. A breathing tube ran from his mouth, and his chest rose up and down with each breath. The crib bars kept me from touching him. Each time we visited I would pray a loud as if we were sitting at the breakfast table. This was all I knew to do. I would then quote, *"This is the day that the Lord has made; we will rejoice* (even in the hospital) *and be glad in it."* Hopefully Stephen would one day understand that every day, no matter what it held, was God's gift and worthy of rejoicing. This "storm" was no different.

Visiting Jeremy's room was similar to Stephen's. He also lay in a hospital bed, encircled by monitors and tubes. His breathing was maintained by a tube like his son's. A CD player had been placed by Jeremy's bed. He had always been a big fan of music. Twice when I visited him, the song "Praise You in the Storm," was playing. I had earlier claimed this song as ours. As with Stephen, all I knew to do and all I could do was pray. I would hold Jeremy's hand and offer up a prayer to the only One who could change things. Praise the Lord that we have a *"Spirit who intercedes for us."* Although my visits and prayers were tear-filled, God was there. His presence filled each room. He understood.

Late Monday I began to notice signs that would usually symbol the beginnings of a miscarriage. In my heart I had expected this but had hung on to hope. Jeremy had been thrilled about this child. I couldn't imagine God letting us find out we were expecting on Friday only to take the baby several days later. My nurse was notified, and I met the hospital Ob-Gyn soon after. They took blood and would inform me in the morning of the results.

Physical therapy became a part of my daily routine. God gave both me and Jeremy incredible physical therapists. Due to the injuries, I could only place weight on my left hand. They took me through the process of getting in a wheelchair step by step. I learned to sit up, scoot over, and transfer using a wooden sliding board. Our sessions were very tiring and sometimes frustrating. Things that were once very easy had become difficult over night. My independence was gone as I relied on at least 2 people to help me. Time and practice would make things much easier.

The same doctor I had earlier met about the pregnancy came by on Tuesday morning. Test results did signal a miscarriage. Procedure required them to take more blood and perform an abdominal ultrasound. The ultrasound was scheduled for sometime Wednesday. We would have to wait and see.

Not long after the doctor's visit, a man and woman knocked on my door and asked if they could see me. They were the parents of the young boy who had hit us. I eagerly said yes. The mother sat beside my bed in tears. If not a word had been spoken, her pain and regret would still have been obvious. Her son had already been forgiven. God's love overflowed to a hurting family like ours. We knew their pain. As best I could I explained mine, Jeremy, and Stephen's injuries. I also told them that we harbored no hard feelings toward their family and begged them to share this with their son. He lay in a hospital room a few doors down from mine and was dealing with injuries of his own. My parents later visited him and personally expressed our feelings. I thanked the Lord for this visit and prayed for a future opportunity to meet this young man myself.

A group of my friends from high school visited Tuesday afternoon. They sat and talked with me for hours. It was great to be removed from the present by remembering the past. We laughed as much as we cried. During this time, Stephen's doctor, the one who had explained things to us in the ICU, came by. He went over the surgery scheduled for 10:30 tomorrow morning.

Another neurosurgeon who specialized in these surgeries had arrived the day before. He now joined their medical team. God was obviously in control. This time, when I asked about the seriousness of the procedure, the doctor said, "It will be okay." I had been waiting to hear these words since our first meeting days ago. Before this doctor left, one of my friends asked if we could pray with him. He agreed. Now I knew, "It would be okay." God's peace filled that room and flooded my heart.

Before going to bed that night, I read some of the comments people had written on our CarePages. These pages and an e-mail update had been set up to keep church members and the community informed. When people wrote encouraging things to us, a copy would be sent to my room.

There was page after page. Each entry lifted my spirits. As I read Tuesday night, Stephen's surgery and our unborn child lay heavy on my heart. One particular comment I read quoted Psalm 27:14 and stood out to me in a special way. *"Wait for the Lord; be strong and take heart and wait for the Lord."* I looked it up in my devotional Bible, which someone had brought from our home earlier that day. As I flipped over to Psalms, I realized that the passage was already bookmarked with a picture of Stephen and Jeremy.

This brought tears to my eyes. Verse 14 was also highlighted. The Holy Spirit then reminded me of something. This verse, the whole chapter, was what I had read the morning of August 27. Twelve hours before our lives were radically changed God had filled my heart with the words of this passage. He knew then what was in store, and He was still in control.

I could vividly see us driving down the road on which the wreck occurred. All day long God had been preparing "our Storm." Like rain in the distance, we were headed right for it. From the family who stopped to help us to the young man who lost control of his vehicle, not one part of this was out of God's hands. He knew every scratch on our bodies. Stephen's surgery was in His design. Though I may not have understood it all, and I may not ever, God was still on His throne. Yes, it was raining hard right now. We were in the middle of the biggest storm of our lives. But God was there. He would be our strength.

4

Wednesday, September 5-Friday, September 7

"In the same way, the Spirit helps us in our weakness. We

do not know what we ought to pray for, but the Spirit

himself intercedes for us with groans that words cannot

express."

-Romans 8:26

The buzz of a cell alarm woke us up at 5:00

Wednesday morning. In order to see Stephen before his

surgery, we had to be in the PICU by 6:00. My nurses had

willingly adjusted their schedules to help with this early

visit. They strapped me in the convertible wheelchair, and

we headed down the hall. Things seemed quieter than

usual, and it was still dark outside. Stephen lay peacefully

in his room. He had no idea what lay ahead of him. In

reality, neither did we. I sobbed a prayer as best I could and

gave our baby to the Lord. We had dedicated him at church

like most parents, but this was for real. Our son's future

was in God's hands. The next few hours would test our faith.

I then visited Jeremy in the ICU. He was resting comfortably. I prayed with him as before. This is what he would have wanted us to do. How deeply I longed for his companionship. How I needed his support during this time. Our son was facing major surgery, and his Daddy had no idea. Praise God that He is there even when we feel all alone.

Morning seemed slower than usual. Breakfast came, but my appetite was weak. I tried to rest some but couldn't fall sleep. Around 11:00, Stephen was taken into surgery. Several hours later a stretcher arrived, and I was taken to another floor of the hospital for my ultrasound. My Mom and Aunt Shirley went with me. I tried to relax as the young nurse rolled the receiver over my stomach. The incisions were still fresh. It seemed to take forever. We weren't given any information as we watched the black and white screen. I imagined several times that I saw something beating.

Without warning, tears began to fall. Jeremy was supposed to be here, I cried. He had been with me during all of Stephen's ultrasounds. Things were so different. I now looked at the screen with fear. As if on cue, my Aunt's cell phone rang. She had forgotten to cut if off. It was our family letting us know that Stephen had successfully came through surgery. He was now in recovery. Praise God that He left me with one of my babies!

Once in my room, Stephen's doctor came by. The surgery had gone well, and he would remain sedated in the PICU for a couple days. Future ramifications from the surgery would be known in the weeks to come. His neck mobility could be an issue. We were just thankful to God for what He had already done.

As the day moved on, I was notified that Jeremy was becoming more coherent. He had opened his eyes once or twice. His mind and body must have been so confused after being asleep for over a week now. The tubes running down his throat became a constant irritation to him. He would chew on them and wrench his face in pain and frustration. The nurses would then have to sedate him even more. His doctors began discussing the option of putting in a trachea. This would be their last resort. Jeremy couldn't come out of the coma if they had to keep sedating him. His body, however, was at least beginning to wake up. We had turned a corner.

Late Wednesday night some of our teens came to visit. They were so excited about how well the first night of student meetings had gone. Our plans had been carried out. The service had taken place in the gym with few glitches. Over 90 students were there! I could hardly wait to share this news with Jeremy!

That first student meeting was only a part of the amazing things God was already doing. I heard stories of many churches around the world who were praying for us. Our alma mater, Liberty, had even held a special prayer meeting. The local Christian radio station was broadcasting our story. The guy who had pulled Stephen from our car at the wreck had begun attending our church. Revival, as we had been praying, was happening. And not just in our church, but in far more hearts than we could have dreamed.

I was shocked to find out on Thursday that the doctors were thinking of releasing me. Most people would be thrilled at this. I didn't feel physically ready. It still took several people to get me in the wheelchair, and I got tired very easily. My injuries had left me completely helpless. Could my family really take care of me without medical assistance? More importantly, could I leave Jeremy and Stephen in that hospital? Here, at least, we were seemingly together. We were seemingly a family. Could I walk in the doors of our home without them? The emotional wounds were deep. The thought of leaving left me feeling scared and alone.

Jeremy and Stephen's conditions remained about the same. Doctors were still anxious to get Jeremy off the breathing tube due to the frustration it was causing him. He wasn't able, however, to adequately follow commands. He was also dealing with a couple infections and a fever that would spike at random. It would take several more days of prayer. Stephen was beginning to open his eyes a little. His breathing tube would also stay in for awhile longer. Both father and son were in similar situations. It was often ironic how much they were alike. If Jeremy had a rough day, Stephen would usually have one. If Jeremy was running a high fever, Stephen would be also. I always knew Stephen was a lot like his Daddy. We prayed they would soon recover together.

The hospital Ob-gyn visited me that afternoon. My room was crowded with people. The results from my latest blood work and ultrasound were in. My levels had continued to drop. The ultrasound found no trace of a baby. It was official that I was miscarrying. I tried to smile as the doctor left and say confidently that God knows best, but I was hurting inside. Life seemed to be going on around me. A miscarriage seemed to be no big deal under the circumstances. But it was. Noticing my eyes tearing up, most everyone left the room. My Mom put her arms around me, and I wept. It wasn't a question of "Why God?" but "How much?".

Later Thursday it was decided that I needed one more night in the hospital. This was a relief. We still didn't know where I would go tomorrow. One of Stephen's nurses mentioned the Ronald McDonald House to us. We had heard of it but didn't know many details. The home was located within walking distance of the hospital. It housed the families of children in the hospital. The purpose was to offer a place of security and rest for hurting parents.

Chances of us getting in were not good. It was the day before I was to be released. I needed a handicap room on the first level. And there was usually a waiting list. My Mom and Brenda went over by faith to meet with the McDonald House staff.

Upon their return, I knew God had done another miracle. They carried a handful of papers. We were in! They had already signed us up. Under the circumstances, they were letting us in last minute. There was even an available handicap room! I was a little skeptical but knew there was no other choice. I definitely didn't want to go home without Jeremy and Stephen. Tomorrow we would move.

Friday afternoon we packed to leave. The pictures and cards were taken down from the walls. It began to look like a hospital room again. My Mom helped me put on "normal clothes" for the first time in almost 2 weeks. On our way out of the room, I finally looked at myself in the mirror. I had refused this until now, being truly scared of what I may see. The reflection looking back at me seemed tired. I literally looked like I had faced death and barely won. Dark circles surrounded my sunken eyes. Fresh scars speckled my left eye and cheek. I barely recognized myself. My spirit seemed stronger but my flesh much weaker.

We visited Jeremy and Stephen on the way out. I told them both bye and that I would only be a brief distance away. Hopefully we would be together again soon. If one was released before the other, he would join me in the Ronald McDonald House. I wanted us to go home as a family like we had come.

Outside I was overwhelmed with the busyness of the world. Cars and people were moving everywhere. The sun was shining full force. Life around us had not stopped just because ours had. A handicap shuttle arrived, and my wheelchair and I were lifted into the back of it. The driver strapped me in for the short distance to the McDonald

House. These shuttles would be our main source of transportation over the next week. Tears came again when I noticed a car seat in the corner of the shuttle. I longed so deeply for Jeremy and Stephen to be with me. Reality continued sinking in.

The Ronald McDonald House proved more than I expected. It was extremely large and included 17 rooms. Ours was on the first level near the kitchen. A large handicap bathroom was on one wall. One bed and a crib were the primary sleeping arrangements. My Mom and I would end up sleeping in the bed. Brenda or my Dad slept on a cot in the floor. If all 4 of us were staying, Brenda would sleep in the crib. This gave us many laughs!

All kinds of food filled the kitchen. Different groups would come in and fix home cooked meals. McDonalds was delivered once a week. We felt very comfortable there and were grateful that God had opened this door. Sometimes we would walk over to the hospital instead of taking the shuttle. It felt so refreshing to be outside. Our days were spent mainly at the hospital. Nights were long and dark. I found myself awake more than I slept. My mind raced. Music was sometimes my only solace as I lay for hours. The group we had heard at the mall on the day of the wreck had released their new CD. Someone brought it to me in the hospital. I nearly wore it out. Each song, in its unique way, ministered to my soul. I couldn't wait to share some of these songs with Jeremy.

5

Saturday, September 8-Sunday, September 9

"But he said to me, 'My grace is sufficient for you, for my power is made perfect in weakness.' Therefore I will boast all the more gladly about my weakness, so that Christ's power may rest on me. That is why, for Christ's sake, I delight in weakness, in insults, in hardships, in persecutions, in difficulties. For when I am weak, then I am strong."

-II Corinthians 12:9,10

After a night of adjusting to our new home, it was time to face the next day. My family felt somewhat refreshed after sleeping in a "normal" bed. The hospital hadn't allowed for much sleep with all the noises and nightly check-ups that had to be done. I remember, for instance, the night when a nurse came by to take out my head staples at midnight. Thankfully, I was wide awake. Being away from this commotion was a welcome relief for all of us. I was very eager, however, to get back over to check on Jeremy and Stephen.

Saturday was juggled between the McDonald House and the hospital. We found the easiest route for walking in case the shuttle was unavailable. The bumpy sidewalks were often painful. It still took 2 people to lift me, and I needed help to do anything. Jeremy remained in the ICU. Doctors talked of removing the breathing tube soon. We prayed they would. He always seemed so uncomfortable. Stephen continued to sleep in the PICU. He would move his arms and legs around at random. We praised the Lord that his injuries had not caused any paralysis. I looked forward to one day seeing him run around our home again. It was hard to imagine me and Jeremy sitting on the couch watching Stephen play like we had done so many times before. The "little things" had become "big dreams" over night. Oh, how we take so much for granted. How we mistake blessings for annoyances. How we see messes instead of grace. Our family would live life differently because of this Storm.

When we awoke Sunday morning, my Mom called the ICU to check on Jeremy. Since it took awhile for me to get ready and over to their rooms, this call became a morning ritual. I was always anxious to hear how my family's night had been. After giving Jeremy's password, Mom handed over the phone. Jeremy's nurse wanted to speak to me directly. The next few words she spoke were the most incredible news I had heard in weeks.

The phrase, "Jeremy ate eggs and bacon" still rings fresh in my ears. My mouth must have dropped. My parents froze when they saw the look on my face. "What?" was the only thing I could muster. When I last saw Jeremy he was still on the breathing tube and incoherent. His nurse must have confused my husband with another patient. But she hadn't. The doctors had decided late Saturday to take a chance and remove Jeremy's breathing tube. If he didn't adjust well, they would do a tracheotomy. All of this had been done without our knowing about it. God knew I could not handle another period of unknown waiting and more procedures. Like a loving Father, He was protecting me. And this morning, September 9, after 13 days in a coma, Jeremy, my love, was awake.

I could have practically jumped out of bed and ran over to the hospital. I had been waiting so long for this moment. In spite of the doctor's unsure diagnosis a week ago, I had faith God's perfect plan would be accomplished. I longed so deeply to see Jeremy's blue eyes. I ached to hear him return the words, "I love you." Our God is so good! I had to see this miracle for myself.

It seemed like ages before we were ready to go over to the hospital. I could hardly wait to see Jeremy. His condition and mental state were somewhat of a concern lingering in the back of my mind. Brain scans had been done last week, and everything looked okay. After almost 2 weeks in a coma, though, Jeremy had to be confused. I prayed God would give me the wisdom to know what to say and when. There were so many things he needed to know.

With every bump of the wheelchair, my heart beat faster. The speeding cars didn't seem that scary anymore. Whatever lay ahead, I knew Jeremy and I could face it together. Once in the hospital, my parents rolled me to the 5th floor. The ICU nurse buzzed over the intercom to let me know it was okay to come in. I had to catch my breath.

There sat Jeremy! His eyes were open! Tubes no longer ran from his throat. The number of monitors even looked less. His head turned back and forth as if attempting to make sense of things. It would take months for me to explain the enormity of all that had happened. For now, though, I just wanted to hear his voice. Beside his bed, I nervously asked, "Jeremy, do you know who I am?" His eyes seemed to look right through me. And with 2 words and his natural sarcasm, "Yes, Tiff," I knew everything would be okay.

For the next while I sat by his bed in my wheelchair. Jeremy only spoke a little and often his words were too quick and quiet to be understood. His parents came in with faces of joy. We shared conversation, but our eyes never left Jeremy. Once he looked over at me, then his Mom, and said to her, "She's hot." I blushed with embarrassment and pride. Yes, my husband was back! Silently I wondered if he would think the same once he saw all my scars. Our love ran much deeper than that!

Jeremy did his best to communicate with us. He was obviously very confused but eager to figure things out. He occasionally dropped jokes that only I would understand. I laughed on the outside while shouting for joy on the inside. God was working. It was now time to check on my other little guy in the PICU.

The waiting room seemed unusually busy outside of Stephen's hall. I wondered if these parents were as broken as I was. Couples embracing each other no longer brought feelings of anger and jealousy. My husband was okay. If able, I knew he would be with me. Even now, he had no idea of the critical condition our son was in. For a few more days, I must face this without him.

Stephen was in his bed but not resting as comfortably as past visits. His sedation seemed to be wearing off. How much longer until he, like his Daddy, would have the breathing tube removed? Like usual, I said our verse and prayed with him. I told him his Daddy was awake and doing better. A doctor came in and cautiously interrupted our visit. He shared with us how they thought Stephen's breathing was improved. They even thought he could begin breathing on his own. Sometime later in the day, Stephen's breathing tube would be removed!

Ecstatic does not begin to sum up the way that I felt. Could God really end this day with both Jeremy and Stephen off their breathing tubes? Would I actually be able to feel Stephen in my arms? I had not held our baby for weeks. In one brief moment, our lives had been changed. Stephen's security, his Daddy and Mommy, had been torn away from him. Holding our son had seemed an impossible dream for weeks now. My eyes overflowed with tears. Dear God, please be with Stephen.

So far the day had been filled with amazement. All the progress had left me thrilled but drained. We headed back over to the McDonald House to rest. The PICU nurse would call us when Stephen's breathing tube was removed. I lay on the bed but as expected, sleep would not come. It seemed like years before the phone finally rang. Stephen's procedure was completed. His breathing tube had been successfully removed!

After getting ready, we headed back over to Stephen's room. He was resting in the little bed. Like his Daddy, his chest no longer raised with the help of a ventilator. Stephen was breathing on his own! Despite the overwhelming desire to whisk him out of that bed into my arms, I refrained. He was resting too peacefully to be bothered. Lord willing tomorrow morning would find him in my embrace!

I said a prayer of thanksgiving to God, and we told Stephen goodnight. On the way back over to the McDonald House, we stopped by the ICU to check on Jeremy. Visiting hours had begun, and we fell in line with other hurting families. Jeremy reclined in his bed wide awake. He seemed happy to see us. I carefully told him of Stephen's improvement. He needed to hear that his son was okay; so many of his unspoken questions were yet to be answered. I could see it in his eyes. After a brief conversation, kiss on the hand, and I love you, we parted ways for the night.

6

Monday, September 10

"Why are you downcast, O my soul? Why so disturbed

within me? Put your hope in God, for I will yet praise him,

my Savior and my God."

-Psalm 42:11

Morning came after another restless night.. In the

wee hours of dawn, my mind wondered from Jeremy to

Stephen. Had I only dreamed that they were both awake?

Would we really be going home soon and joining the ranks

of a family again? God had been so good!

In the middle of getting ready, my Mom's cell

phone rang. I could tell by her voice that she was talking to

a stranger. We had met many new people recently, and I

imagined who it could possibly be. After a few moments

she hung up and explained to me the opportunity that had

just been offered. One of the local news stations that had

been covering our story wanted to interview me. The

reporter, a young woman, was calling for permission to come out. She had shared with my Mom the tremendous interest and feedback our wreck had received. The community, she said, needed an update. They were eager to hear from someone in the family.

What an unusual way to start the day. I had figured our family was old news by now. I never dreamed that people still cared, especially those in the community whom neither Jeremy nor I knew. My mind went back and forth. I should do this interview because: people wanted to hear from me, Jeremy would want me to, our church family and especially our teenagers needed to see that I was okay, God had opened up another door of ministry to us. I shouldn't do this interview because: my plate was already full with visits to the hospital, being in the spotlight was not top on my agenda, who am I to represent our God to such a large audience.

Mom had told the reporter we would call her back later in the day. I had several hours to pray about it. For now, we would get ready and head over the hospital like usual. Jeremy and Stephen needed me focused and joyful for them. A decision would be made later.

On the way over to the hospital that morning an older gentleman stopped my Mom as she pushed the wheelchair. We had never seen him before. He looked me in the eyes and said that God had told him something special would happen to him that day, and he believed I was it. I was shocked and a little confused. He asked me what I was doing there and what had caused all my casts. I briefly explained our family's situation, and he wrote down our names on a piece of paper. He then promised to pray for us. As this unique conversation ended, the man said a phrase to me that I will never forget. His words, "Young lady, you wear Jesus well," have challenged me ever since our providential meeting. This stranger encouraged me that day in ways he will never know. I again realized this Storm was all about Christ.

With my soul still stirred, we made our way to Jeremy's room. He lay wide awake with his eyes fixed on the TV that had earlier been rolled beside his bed. As expected, a sporting event filled the screen. Both us had always been big sports fans. Most of our weeknights were spent at ballgames. Until this year I had coached the school's volleyball team. Wanting to spend more time with our family, I had hesitantly given this position over to someone else. Jeremy had also relinquished some of his soccer coaching due to other priorities. Even in these decisions made months ago, God was working. Both sports' seasons were almost complete, and we had only been to two games. In just a couple months, basketball season would begin. Jeremy had planned on coaching the boys, and they had been preparing all summer. I wondered if he would still want to do this. I wondered if he would be able.

The doctors came in on their morning visit to see how the night had treated Jeremy. After checking his vitals, they informed us that he was finally strong enough to undergo the two surgeries they had been putting off. The first, to correct his broken wrist, would take place tomorrow. I immediately began wondering how he would be put to sleep. Would a breathing tube once again have to be inserted? If so, would Jeremy endure the same complications as before and go into another coma? From their present standpoint, the doctors were convinced a breathing tube was the only way to go. I offered a silent prayer, "Please, Lord, work this out."

At the insistence of the nurse maintaining visiting hours, my parents pushed my wheelchair to the 6th floor. I was anxious to see Stephen and prayed once again that I could hold him. If he was resting, I told myself, I would leave him be. When the PICU door opened, it was clear that Stephen was wide awake and very uncomfortable.

A nurse was in his room, and Stephen wiggled in the arms of a close friend of ours, Judy. Seeing us, she graciously stood up and handed me my baby. My arms were outstretched and eagerly waiting. With only one good arm, I did my best to hold the squirming little boy. He flung himself everywhere. I could barely control him. The feeding tube made him difficult to maneuver. His cry was very raspy and constant. The breathing tube had scratched his throat. I held him close and quietly sang one of our favorite songs in his ear. For a few brief seconds he lay still and listened. The small room grew silent. My world stopped. I was holding Stephen.

For as long as I possibly could, I held him. Stephen was in obvious pain. His eyes held the same confusion as his Daddy's. The amazing moment of holding him was darkly overshadowed by his cries. I was helpless. For the next few months, Jeremy and I would not be able to care for our son. We could barely care for ourselves. Looking deeply into Stephen's eyes, I barely recognized our son. He had grown so much. His face looked stiff and tired. One eye seemed to pull inward toward his nose. The ring of his screams filled the room and implanted themselves in my heart. Oh God, I know Your will is perfect. Please comfort our son while we can't.

With a thankful yet heavy heart we left Stephen's room. I had a lot to think about. At the time of our wreck, Stephen had been very attached to me. Strangers made him uneasy. I could only imagine how scared he must be with all the doctors and nurses coming in. Someone, I decided, would have to begin staying with him 24 hours a day until he was able to go home. As much as I wanted to, my better judgment told me that I could not be that person. My heart desperately longed to be Stephen's comfort, but I knew it was impossible. Very quickly, God gave me two couples who loved our son and would be perfect "substitute parents."

The first whom I asked to stay with Stephen were a retired couple in our church, Joe and Judy. Judy was the one who was holding Stephen when I visited earlier in the day. She and Joe wanted to help. Stephen loved both of them and had stayed at their house often. With high hopes, I dialed their number and spoke to Joe. He graciously agreed. Over the next week, this dear couple would put their lives on hold and stay with Stephen each day.

Secondly, I asked Daren and Kim to stay with Stephen. Over the past year, this couple and their two teenage boys had become our closest friends. They loved our son like their own. They also willingly agreed to begin staying with Stephen. Due to work, they would have to take the night shift. For over a week, this family sacrificed for us and endured many sleepless nights in the hospital.

We could not have made it through our Storm without these dear friends. They were for Stephen what we could not be during a time when he needed his Daddy and Mommy most. God had put them in our lives for a purpose. No amount of thank you's could truly express how indebted we are to them for their sacrifice. Knowing they were with Stephen put both mine and Jeremy's minds at ease. We were able to heal quicker knowing that our son was not alone.

Later on in the day, I made the decision to do the news interview. I didn't know what I would say, but I was confident this was part of God's plan. Mom called the reporter back, and we set up a time for the following night. They would come to the McDonald House to make things easier for me. I put this in the back of my mind. There were more important things going on in the present.

After a short rest, our evening was spent at the hospital. Jeremy seemed more coherent and aware of his surroundings. He had even recognized one of our teenagers earlier in the day. His imminent surgery, however, was not mentioned. We could discuss that with him tomorrow. Stephen appeared a little more comfortable than he had that morning. He still cried more than I had ever heard him in the previous 16 months of his life. Daren and Kim were there and ready to stay the night. I left him in their care and resting in the arms of our Savior. His Creator would better comfort him than I ever could.

7

Tuesday, September 11

"The Lord is my light and my salvation-whom shall I fear?

The Lord is the stronghold of my life-of whom shall I be

afraid? For in the day of trouble he will keep me safe in his

dwelling; he will hide me in the shelter of his tabernacle

and set me high upon a rock. I am still confident of this: I

will see the goodness of the Lord in the land of the living. "

-Psalm 27:1,5,13

15 days since the wreck, and time to face another day. Lord willing, Jeremy would successfully undergo his surgery, and we would have only one more to go. Lord willing, Stephen would be more content and closer to moving to a regular room. Lord willing, I would represent my family and our God well tonight during the interview.

This particular morning, Stephen seemed about the same. Joe and Judy were "on duty," and reported from Daren and Kim that he had barely slept the night before.

We were all becoming more and more convinced that the feeding tube running from his nose was causing him a great deal of frustration. I asked his nurse about this, and she explained that the tube would stay until Stephen was drinking and eating sufficiently on his own. Starting today, those staying with him would begin offering him liquids from his sippy cup. When bringing familiar things from home to him earlier in our stay, his favorite cup had been brought. I prayed he would easily take his juice, quickly advance to food, and the feeding tube would be removed. Another obstacle lay in our path toward home.

Knowing it was getting close to Jeremy's surgery time, we rushed over to the ICU. Mom called in and told the nurses we were there to see Jeremy. In utter disbelief, we were told that he had already been taken. They had come more than two hours early. Fears about the breathing tube began to fill my mind. What if? I had not seen my husband or even had a chance to share with him what was being done. He must have left that room so confused, once again. What do we do now? Where do we go? We headed down the hall in frustration. A silent prayer once again filled my heart, "Please, God, just let me see him."

As quickly as possible with a wheelchair, we found the surgical waiting room. The large room was crowded. Jeremy's Mom, who had met us at the ICU, checked us in at the registration desk. Taking a chance, she asked the secretary if we could somehow see Jeremy. Her reply, "No, he's already been taken back," came as no surprise. The surgery would take a couple of hours, and I knew I could not sit in my wheelchair that long. I would wait in the McDonald House until Jeremy's Mom called with news.

On our way out, I was still a little in the flesh and angry. "God, I just wanted to see Jeremy for one second before His surgery. After all we've been through…" Not 10 steps outside the waiting room door and 10 seconds into my silent pity party, we were almost ran over by a nurse. She was practically running through the hall and looked about as flustered as us. I quickly recognized her as one of Jeremy's nurses. She must have somewhere important to go.

Once again I could hardly believe what I was hearing. She immediately, in a rushed tone, began explaining to us that *we* were the ones she was looking for. When Jeremy was taken to surgery early, she was his nurse. Knowing we would want to see him, this dear lady had begun searching the halls in hopes that she would run into someone from his family. In mid-sentence she told us to follow her, and we flew through the hospital quicker than ever.

We wound our way through several hallways and stopped at two large, metal doors. With a push of the button, we were in and standing beside Jeremy. The nurse left, and my Mom went to get Jeremy's Mom. The look on my face must have confused Jeremy even more. I was still in shock. In spite of all my complaining, God had let me see Jeremy! But wasn't that like Him? In spite of our sin, He loved us and gave us His Son. What love and grace! In spite of our unworthiness, He was using our family. He had chosen each of us to go through this Storm. God was doing amazing things…miracles in front of our own eyes. In that huge hospital, how could that nurse have found us? How had our paths crossed? God is so big. Father, I whispered, forgive me for limiting You to my finite mind.

It ended up being awhile before Jeremy was taken into surgery. We stayed and talked with him in this pre-op room for over an hour. When the anesthesiologist came in, she began talking about the process they would use to put Jeremy to sleep. Once again, a breathing tube would be inserted, and fear entered my heart. I signed the papers as best I could with my left hand and refocused on Jeremy.

Soon after, this same anesthesiologist came back over to Jeremy's bedside. We assumed they were ready to take him into surgery. Surprisingly, after further review of Jeremy's paperwork, the decision had been made that a breathing tube would not be inserted. Instead, he would be given a local anesthetic and something to relax him. Relief filled my heart. Our fears of his past reaction to the breathing tube had been in vain. Had we already forgotten Who was in control?

Jeremy was taken back into surgery, and I returned to the Ronald McDonald House for some rest. After hours of waiting and prayer, we received the phone call that Jeremy had successfully come through his surgery. The once badly broken wrist had been set with a plate and several screws. For days I had watched that wrist and his fingers swell. It was almost like a balloon was gradually being blown up. The anticipation of seeing his hand corrected gave me something to look forward to. Jeremy was making progress.

Around 5:00 that evening, the local news media showed up. Their crew consisted of a cameraman and reporter. The reporter was one of the most attractive young women I had ever seen in person. Exactly what one would expect! I thought, Jeremy's gonna be so jealous! In preparation, I had only washed and dried my hair. After the insistence of others to put on some makeup we compromised with lip-gloss. My first television appearance would be done in a new pair of striped pajama pants and a white t-shirt. I had no energy to spend on "getting beautiful" and reminded myself this wasn't about me. May God's love and beauty flow through me from my heart.

The interview went well. I felt very comfortable sitting in that rocking chair talking about what had happened. Sharing our injuries came naturally, and I felt in my heart that God would give me more chances to share in the future. This was part of the preparation process. A smile stayed on my face as I explained what God had done for each member of our family. His plans are always best.

As the interview concluded, and the small crew prepared to leave, I asked, "Why did you do this? People have wrecks all the time. What is so different about ours?" She explained again how the response they had received about our story had been overwhelming. I smiled knowing God had opened this door. Tonight, once again, was His doing. As they walked down the porch steps, the reporter looked at me smiling and said, "You're so happy. I need to catch some of those vibes." And I wanted to say, "It's the Holy Spirit and pure grace."

Once the interview was done, we ate a quick supper. Although the church was bringing the most delicious meals, my appetite stayed small. How could I eat with Jeremy and Stephen unable to? Maybe our visit to Stephen's room would show his appetite and chances of losing the feeding tube better.

Jeremy had been placed back in the ICU to recover and wait for his surgery the following day. He seemed about the same as he had that morning. His eyes were still fixed on the small TV screen. The left hand was bandaged but already looking more human than it had in the weeks before. I imagined the physical therapy that must lay ahead for all 3 of us-one more surgery to go. We spent some time talking to Jeremy. He only spoke a little and in a whisper we could barely understand. The breathing tube from weeks before had made his throat sore and raspy. I would be glad to see and hear him more like his old self, yet I wondered if any of us would ever be the same.

Stephen's room was next to visit. Joe and Judy were switching shifts with Daren and Kim. Judy reported that although they had brought Stephen food, he had refused to eat. Based on the leftovers sitting on a tray in the corner, I understood why. As a 16 month old, Stephen was already as picky as his parents. A small menu lay under the supper tray and to get my mind off Stephen's helpless cries, I began looking at it. This menu contained all of Stephen's food choices for the following day. My Aunt Brenda grabbed a pen and began to check off the items I thought Stephen might eat. In a small way I began to feel like his Mother again. I was making some choices that would hopefully push us closer to home.

Judy did report that Stephen had drunk a little, though. He refused his sippy cup but drank a little from a juice box. It definitely wasn't enough, but it was a start. I thanked God for those few sips. I had no idea the days of waiting and hoping he would eat that lay before us. I touched Stephen's hand and told him I loved him before we left. Oh, to take him home and hold him in my arms!

The interview was aired that night while I avoided watching it until the next morning. Everyone said it was good. I wondered what Jeremy would think when he saw it in the future. It seemed best that he not even know for now.

I didn't want him to have some confused idea that I was out being on TV while he lay in the hospital. Nothing could be farther from the truth. Hopefully I had made a wise decision, and he would be proud. Hopefully God would continue strengthening our family and using us as He had planned.

8

Wednesday, September 12

"But let all who take refuge in you be glad; let them ever sing for joy. Spread your protection over them, that those who love your name may rejoice in you. For surely, O Lord, you bless the righteous; you surround them with your favor as with a shield."

-Psalm 5:11,12

A new day came holding one final surgery for Jeremy. After a quick visit to his room, he was once again taken back. This time they would be repairing his right heel. In addition to breaking his left foot, the heel of his right has been completely crushed during the wreck. The doctors had warned us that it was one of the worst breaks you could have, and one of the most painful recoveries to endure. They even admonished us that Jeremy's walking could forever be effected.

In answer to prayer, another anesthetic was given, and Jeremy avoided the breathing tube I so dreaded. We would wait a couple of hours to see how things went. Our visit to Stephen's room showed no major change from the day before. He still seemed very restless. I shuttered seeing the formula being pumped into his feeding tube. For the first year of his life I had chosen to nurse our son and give him what I had read was the best possible nutrition for an infant. It seemed that all the work had been in vain. But even this was part of God's plan, and I was learning to trust Him. For now, Stephen's main source of nutrition would have to be the small bag of formula hanging beside his bed. Please, son, eat something!

Before leaving his room that day, I made a decision. For days now, the large neck brace Stephen wore looked big and awkward to us all. It often slid up and over his mouth. The sides of his neck were red and raw. It had cost $1000 and had been flown in from another state right after his surgery. Still, I knew in my heart, that it was not the right size for him. Stephen had always been small. I made a vow to myself and our helpless son that I would do something about this. Wherever we had to go and whatever we would have to pay were no option. If Stephen had to live with this brace for the next 12 weeks, it needed to fit. Something had to stop the crying.

Once back at my temporary home, we began another wait for that "out of surgery" phone call. Soon a cell phone rang, but it was not Jeremy's Mom as I had suspected. Instead a woman named Suzanne's voice came through the speaker. Tears welled up in my Mom's eyes as she listened to this stranger's words.

Suzanne, whom I did not remember, had been on the scene of the wreck. She and her family had arrived before any medical help. She was the nurse I had heard about and longed to meet. Suzanne's breath was what had given Stephen his life back. How desperately I just wanted to say thank you. Those 2 words, though, have never seemed enough.

I eagerly told Mom that yes, I wanted to meet her. Mom already knew this answer. We had been talking about this young nurse for weeks now. Did I feel like I was ready yet? No, not really, but the desire to say thank you was greater than the fear of hearing the story one more time. Suzanne wanted to see Stephen. She needed to. Every time she heard a siren, the image of Stephen and the smells of the scene flooded her mind. To erase this personal pain, she needed to see him herself. She longed to hold him in his present condition, not the one that often filled her memory.

While we had greatly limited Stephen's visitors to a few close family and friends, I urged Suzanne to go and see him. That was the least I could do. After her visit to his room, she would then come and see me. Within an hour, I would be meeting one of our angels.

Finally the phone call that we were originally waiting for came. Jeremy had successfully made it through surgery. His heel had been repaired. To our surprise, he would not be returning to the ICU. Instead, after recovery, he would be moved to a step down unit called Acute Care. I had spent one night there myself. This new room would be located a few doors down from the regular room where I had spent over a week. I prayed he would have some of the same nurses I did. Here, at least, we would have more flexible and lengthy visiting hours. This was definite progress.

Before going back over to the hospital that evening, a knock came on the room door. I knew it was Suzanne. I had been waiting. I'm not sure if I have ever hugged anyone with such love as I hugged Suzanne that day. In one unexpected moment, two strangers' lives had been forever knit together. I had so much to say, so many questions to ask, but all I could do was cry. How could I ever say thank you?

Suzanne, and everyone else in the room that afternoon, was as emotional as myself. We listened as Suzanne explained how she, her husband, John, and their 3 young children had come upon our wreck. They had stayed late at their daughter's riding lessons and were traveling home that day nearly an hour later than usual. Driving up on both vehicles, they immediately stopped. John was a retired highway patrolman and had seen many wrecks like ours before. He sent Suzanne over to Stephen while he headed to our car. In his mind, he was protecting his wife from the sight of the 2 corpses he suspected he would find. There was no way anyone could have survived, he assumed.

At this point, David held unconscious Stephen in his arms. Explaining she knew CPR, Suzanne took our limp son into her arms. She laid him on the ground across the street from both cars and began CPR. At first, she explained, there was no pulse. She kept trying. Soon another nurse arrived on the scene and began assisting her. After a few more moments and a few more breaths, Suzanne felt a pulse. Soon after, came the cry all the onlookers had been waiting for. As she stood up and handed Stephen to a fireman, she realized the number of people that had surrounded her. It was strange, she said, as she hadn't seen any of them. All her focus had been on our son.

During this time, while her kids obediently waited in their car, John climbed in the backseat with us. As she explained the details John had shared with her, something in my mind clicked. Her husband was the only stranger whom I remembered from the scene. For weeks now, I had been trying to figure out who this unknown hero was. John had kept both Jeremy and I calm. He had wiped the blood from my eyes. I would never forget the role he played that day. I couldn't wait to see John again face to face and under different circumstances.

Suzanne then explained how it had always been her dream to become a nurse. Recently, she had finished nursing school but had not passed her final bar by a few points. Discouraged, she had given up on her goal. After resuscitating Stephen that afternoon, however, she now had the confidence to push forward. She would take the test again and in the future become a Registered Nurse.

Pride filled my heart as I realized how God was using Stephen. While he struggled in his little room, God had been and was still using him. How humbled I was that God already had His hand on our son. What responsibility lay ahead of us as parents! In what other ways would God use Stephen? I made a mental note to share Suzanne's story with Jeremy soon.

After more hugs and tears, Suzanne left. Our story was coming together piece by piece each day. My soul was bursting with gratefulness. We spent the rest of the evening at the hospital with Jeremy and Stephen. Acute Care found Jeremy awake and looking around at his new surroundings. The large room held four beds, each separated by curtains. Jeremy lay in the back corner. He seemed a little dazed still from his earlier surgery. To my relief, one of my favorite nurses would be his nurse this first night. It gave us comfort knowing her and knowing that she already knew our situation. She had shed many tears in my room during previous weeks. I knew she would take good care of Jeremy.

A brief visit to Stephen's room (His cries always forced me to leave quickly. I felt so helpless and heartbroken each time.), and night was upon us. I reminded Mom of my plans about Stephen's neck brace, and we promised each other we would take care of it first thing tomorrow. My mind raced as I played out the last 12 hours. It had been a good day but an emotional day. I was broken yet rejoicing at the powerful hand of God. Our family was

broken yet healing a little more each day. God was making

all things new.

9

Thursday, September 13-Friday, September 14

"Because of the Lord's great love we are not consumed, for his compassions never fail. They are new every morning; great is your faithfulness."

-Lamentations 3:22,23

Same routine and plan as the days before lay ahead of us the following sunny morning. Jeremy seemed much more aware than he had been before when we visited his room. His voice was still weak, but he was talking more. I could tell he was very confused. For the first time, Jeremy asked us if he could go home. By that night, he was insisting he go home. We did our best to explain that he needed more time to heal. His concept of time had been very distorted. He often invited visitors to revival not realizing it had ended over a week ago. Jeremy's mind remembered the wreck, but he had no recollection of the coma he had lain in. He thought it was Tuesday, only a day after the wreck.

I desperately wanted to explain things to him. We had so much to share. Being careful, though, and not knowing how much he could handle at this point, I only answered questions he asked. God would give us time in the days ahead. Patience would have to be on my side.

Surprisingly, Stephen's neurosurgeon was in his room that morning when we visited. I had not seen him in a couple days. It was not often that we visited at the same time. He reported that from a neurological standpoint, Stephen was doing well. He still, however, would have to begin drinking and eating before he could go home.

Yesterday's decision about Stephen's oversized neck brace came to my mind, and I shared my concerns with his doctor. He agreed, and I asked where we needed to go to get a custom-fit one. From his pocket he pulled out a business card and handed it to me. There was a specialist in the area who could do this for Stephen. If I gave him a call, we could set up an appointment.

I was thrilled! We didn't have to travel a long distance or board a plane. This specialist was nearby. I would give him a call first thing when we returned to the McDonald House.

Stephen's Dr. left, and I looked at the business card in my hand. What an answer to prayer, I thought. Not a minute later, the room door flew open again. A man dressed in a white doctor's coat came around the corner and shook my hand. As he introduced himself to all of us in the room, my mouth dropped open. Tears of joy began to fill my eyes. I froze. In my mind I repeated the man's name and looked again at the business card I had just been given. This was the same man! This was the neck brace specialist Stephen's doctor had just told me about!

After regaining my composure and realizing the confused stare this doctor was giving me, I snapped back into reality. How did he get here? In answer to my unasked question, the man explained how he had ran into Stephen's doctor in the hall, and he had sent him to our room. In his hand, he held a bag full of infant neck braces. Within 5 minutes Stephen had a new and custom designed neck brace! His mouth would no longer slip below the pads, and the rubbed spots could heal. I was overwhelmed by this miracle! It was one of the biggest "Wow!" moments of my entire life!

Later that afternoon I began feeling very queasy. Any sight of food made my stomach turn. I prayed it was just my nerves and not some kind of sickness. We had avoided this so far but realized how weak my immune system must be. The call that both Joe and Judy were sick along with my Dad only confirmed what I had suspected. As I hugged the toilet that night from my wheelchair, I continued to realize God's perfect plan in taking the baby. With every cough my stomach pulled at the fresh incision, my back ached, and my throat burned from the breathing tube. Had this pregnancy been like Stephen's, I may have found myself in this condition more than not. My mind could not fathom dealing with the nausea along with everything else on our plate. As much as I hurt from the miscarriage, I knew God's plans were perfect.

The amount of medicine I could take was very limited. I was already taking more pills than ever before in my life. Jeremy had always hated taking medicine, so I wondered how he would do with this. Even in the ICU after he first woke up, he had gotten sick from some liquid he had been given. The Lord would have to work even in this small area.

Jeremy and I were also both required to take shots each morning and night. With our confinement to the wheelchair, blood clots were a constant concern. My Mom had learned to give me mine, and I knew Jeremy's brother David would be willing to give Jeremy his. As much as the shots stung, Mom and I admittedly laughed numerous times at her giving me shots. I would often yell, "Take it out!" just to remind her how much pain she was causing me! The first time she even tried, I cried out as she rubbed the alcohol swab before the needle was even inserted. We and all the nurses in the room laughed as Mom jumped back in shock. God gave comical times amidst all the pain. Sometimes you have to choose to see grace!

Even after much insistence, I never let myself take a nerve pill. Often at nights the idea was very tempting. My mind would not rest even though my body had collapsed in the bed. Not because of conviction, these pills are often a gift from God, but because of pure determination, I always said no. The stubbornness in me explained how I wanted to say that God got me through all this without the help of any technique He had given mankind. By His grace, we made it through.

By Friday morning, the nausea was mostly gone. I prayed no one else, especially Jeremy would get sick. It was suspected that maybe Stephen had already had it as he had been a little sick the day before. I personally thought it was coming from the large amount of formula they were pumping into his body.

When we visited his room, he was sitting in Joe's arms facing a young woman. She was his physical therapist and would be working with him each day until he went home. There was so much he would have to relearn from sitting up to walking. His muscles, like ours, had become weak from lying in his hospital bed. We would be taking home an infant in a 17 month old's body. I often wondered how many children have ever had to learn to walk two times.

Stephen was much calmer today than in the past. He was, however, a little uneasy with his therapist (as he was with any stranger who came into his room). I shuddered a little watching his helpless body propped against Joe. We would need a lot of help in the weeks to come. Stephen would require constant attention. His eyes followed a little ball from side to side. With the neck brace, he was unable to turn his head at all. I prayed he would somehow get more than the 50% movement doctors expected he would always have. Therapy and time would be vital.

The little feeding bag seemed more full this morning than usual. Stephen's nurse came in and explained how they had upped the amount of formula he was receiving. His body was now receiving way more than I knew it could handle. What could I say? His therapist left, and my assumptions were confirmed as Stephen began to get sick once again. I knew it could be the bug we had all gotten, but in my heart I felt it was the increase of formula. When his nurse came back in I explained this to her. As always, she listened and took the information I shared with her back to Stephen's doctor.

Again I began to cry. I always felt so vulnerable sitting in that wheelchair. I wondered how much people truly believed what I told them. Yes, I did have a lot to deal with, but I wasn't too overwhelmed to think clearly about my husband and son. I knew them better than anyone else. Our God only knows the helplessness I often felt. His grace gave me courage to speak up on their behalf even through the fear.

Thankfully Stephen's formula intake was reduced that afternoon. He did not get sick again. Deep in my heart I remembered that God hears when we feel no one else does. He understands our feelings; even when human words cannot express them. He had watched His own Son suffer, so I knew He understood even greater the pain that often filled my heart. He was listening to every thought I felt, and I hoped my heart was listening to Him.

Jeremy was continuing to improve in his Acute Care room. Always being a friendly person, he now called his nurses by name. I smiled as they kindly responded to his requests. Beside his bed lay a little blue breathing mechanism, the same that I had been given weeks before. I remembered the nurses' explanations of how important it was to use the machine several times each day. Those deep breaths would keep the lungs open and hopefully prevent pneumonia from setting in. My Dad had challenged me to blowing contests back when I lay where Jeremy was. He would blow in the tube and then I would. My goal was always to beat him, which never happened. My personal best had been reaching the 2,000 mark.

I asked Jeremy if he had been using his breathing tube, and he said no. His brother, David, reminded him how he needed to be using it often. Jeremy shook him off but took the tube in his hands. He gave a pitiful little blow and the measurement bubble barely moved. Jeremy laid it back down in frustration. I then gave him a challenge I knew he couldn't resist.

Jeremy had always been so competitive. Part of what drew us to each other back in college was our desire to compete and win. He would not like the thought of me being better than him at something, even this little breathing machine! I took his tube off the table and explained how I could reach 2,000. Nu-uh he told me, so I had to prove him wrong. With all my breath, I blew and with crossed-eyes watched the little bubble rise to 2,000. Jeremy stared at me. He then quickly took the tube, inhaled, and blew as hard as he could. The little lever trembled and rose to 500 before falling again. David and I immediately began bragging on Jeremy. It was a huge deal that he had even attempted the thing, much less got it to move. I knew, though, that my 2,000 would be beaten in the next few days!

The "when can I go home" questions unexpectedly began to come from Jeremy's lips again. We had all been wondering the same thing. More importantly for now, we wanted to know when he could be moved to a regular room. He, in our opinion, was ready, and I longed for open visiting hours.

David spoke with Jeremy's nurse about this, and surprisingly, we were told that the doctors had already been considering it. From a medical standpoint, he was ready for this step-down. Their only holdback, however, was Jeremy's mental state. He still had his days confused and often said things that didn't make complete sense. His doctors were worried about him being alone in a room 24 hours a day. If we, as Jeremy's family, could assure them he would have someone constantly with him, they would let him move in the next couple days.

As we left, the "cast guy" came in to fit Jeremy. He would have a cast on his left arm and one on both his left and right feet. As expected, he chose Carolina blue for all 3. I had 2 casts myself (pink and blue) and could not imagine having another. My upper left leg was weak enough from the broken femur without having a heavy cast on it. Both Jeremy's femurs had been broken, and now he would have a cast at the bottom of each one. I prayed he would not be too uncomfortable or in much pain. Regardless, we were another step closer to home.

10

Saturday, September 15-Sunday, September 16

"For my thoughts are not your thoughts, neither are your ways my ways," declares the Lord. As the heavens are higher than the earth, so are my ways higher than your ways and my thoughts than your thoughts."
–Isaiah 55:8,9

After waking up Saturday and receiving my Mom-Brenda duo sponge bath, they backed my wheelchair up to the sink. The huge handicap accessible bathroom had been a tremendous blessing. While in the past I "had" to wash my hair each morning, I now felt refreshed when it got clean every other day. It was such a hassle and in the scheme of things, not that important. At first, we all 3 would be soaked including the entire bathroom floor and about 5 towels. The process had just recently gotten easier. Today, September 15, was hair washing day.

Being careful around my scalp where the staples had been, my 2 caretakers quickly washed my hair. Usually they would blow dry it for me, and I would watch in the mirror. My right arm was in the cast, and my left had become too weak to hold the dryer. This morning, though, I decided to try it myself. I took the dryer from Mom and for the first time since the morning of August 27, I dried my own hair! Admittedly, it was very exciting for all of us! I ached for some taste of independence. I wanted to do something on my own. This was my start! I even figured out a new way of flipping it so the scabs in my scalp no longer showed. How trivial yet encouraging the morning had started!

To my surprise, God had even more exciting things in store this day than my hair drying. When we visited Stephen's room, we were delighted to hear that he had drunk and eaten a little! At this point, no one cared how much! We were all just excited that he was getting his appetite back. It would take a few more weeks for it to fully return, but Stephen was on his way. I tried to hold him and tell him how proud Mommy was that he had eaten, but again he proved too strong for my weak body. Judy graciously accepted him from my arms, and his crying stopped.

I often wondered why Stephen cried each time he saw me, or when I tried to hold him. Satan would often say it was because Stephen blamed me for what had happened; that in some terrible way Jeremy and I were punishing him. The Holy Spirit would slip in and silence these thoughts. In my soul I felt Stephen wanted me. He could not, I assumed, understand why I couldn't get up and walk with him-Why I was in that wheelchair and both my arm and leg were in casts. My presence must have often confused him. Even that day as I left with questions in my mind, I rejoiced. Stephen was eating!

On our way to visit Jeremy we ran into his Mom. She excitedly told us that earlier this morning, Jeremy had been moved to a regular room. He was still on the 11th floor but was in a visit-anytime room of his own!

It was a thrill to see Jeremy lying in these new surroundings! He even seemed more comfortable and like himself. The small room looked almost identical to the one I had been in. It had a window, several chairs, and a TV, which was presently playing sports (as it would practically the whole time Jeremy stayed there!). His Mom had already begun hanging family pictures and cards on the wall.

Jeremy smiled as we came in. Mom rolled my wheelchair beside his bed, and Jeremy asked me for a kiss. Our lips barely touched through the rails of the hospital bed. His dirty hair and unwashed face mattered nothing to me. This was my husband, and I was overwhelmed with gratitude at how far he had come. I was proud of him and the spiritual strength that had proven itself so strong. We were becoming a couple again!

We watched a little TV together like old times. I couldn't get up and fold clothes, though, like I had done in the past. It was me and him, with nowhere to go and nothing to do! Our Moms even left the room, so we could have a little personal time together. This was a first in almost 3 weeks. He asked me about Stephen, and I carefully explained again that Stephen was still in the hospital. He remembered Stephen being unconscious on the accident scene. I assured him our son was making progress. He desperately wanted to see him. Jeremy never asked about the unborn baby I had been carrying. I said nothing and prayed for the perfect time. Our church, friends, and even the media wanted to know if I was still pregnant. I refused to tell anyone until Jeremy knew. For now, I would continue bearing this alone.

Several visitors came in and spoke with me and Jeremy. We were surprised at the number of people who even that day stopped their busy schedules to come and see us. So many times we would cry as prayers were sent up on our behalf. While exhausted, Jeremy and I were grateful to know people still cared. This was only the beginning.

Night quickly came with little sleep, and we were awakened by God's beautiful sunlight. I thought about the blessings of the day before and wondered what the next few hours had in store. We visited Jeremy first as I was excited to see how his first night in the regular room had gone. His companion that first night had been his Mom, and I could tell by her tired eyes that things had not gone too smoothly. While better than the Acute Care, nurses still came in at all hours to check and re-check Jeremy. In addition to this, Jeremy had been sick on his stomach. He, like Stephen, was learning to get his appetite back. Jeremy barely ate, and when he did, it usually would not stay down. His stomach had a lot of adjusting to do.

Again, as a concerned father, Jeremy asked about Stephen. He desperately wanted to see him. I fearfully was not sure if he was really ready for this. I remembered my shock at seeing Stephen for the first time after his surgery. I had hardly recognized him. For Jeremy, it had been 20 days since he had seen our son. But today, there was no discussion to be had. It was time.

Jeremy had been doing physical therapy for a couple days now, but he was still not strong enough to endure a wheelchair. His main goal had been to sit up on the side of his bed. Visiting Stephen's room was an impossibility. We would somehow have to bring Stephen to him.

With this goal in sight, my Mom pushed me to the elevator and down to Stephen's room. Stephen had done okay the night before and slept for a couple of hours.

Again, we were looking for any type of progress. With his nurses' help, we quickly had a plan as to how we would reunite Jeremy and Stephen.

I would remain in my wheelchair, and Stephen, Lord-willing, would sit on my lap. For the short amount of time we would be gone, his feeding tube would be unplugged. That way we didn't have to pull anything behind us. This was a huge blessing.

As they placed Stephen in my arms, I prayed he would actually let me hold him. He was much easier to manage without the wires running everywhere. We were pushed down the hallway and out of the children's unit of the hospital. My heart longed for the day we did this and did not have to return. For over a week now, I had passed people taking their children home. I could see the joy on their faces. When, my heart asked, would this be us?

The entire way up to Jeremy's room, Stephen sat still. He looked around as best he could and seemed to be taking in his surroundings. His ICU room and the one he now lay in had been his home for too long. He was enjoying the change of scenery. For the next 5 minutes or so, I was finally able to hold our baby. It has been so long. My kisses covered his forehead as nothing mattered in those moments but us. I could have held him for days.

Sooner than I'd have selfishly liked, we came to Jeremy's door. This was a huge moment. How would Jeremy react? Was he truly ready for this? As we opened the door, our family was instantaneously reunited. The 3 of us were together, finally in the same room. God was lovingly restoring our family. Immediately, Jeremy put his arms out for Stephen. Joe took him from my arms and placed him in his Daddy's.

Stephen squirmed and, much like myself, Jeremy tried his best to comfort him. I could see both joy and concern filling Jeremy's eyes. After a moment, Stephen was returned to me. Jeremy had many questions but was very positive. I explained the neck brace to him and told him what the purpose of the tubes were. As quickly as we came, Stephen was returned his own room. We had strict orders to bring him back as quickly as possible.

In the later hours of that day, Jeremy began to deal more deeply with issues that he had harbored in his mind. Seeing Stephen made things more real. He realized our son's life had forever been changed. Over and over Jeremy told me and his Mom that he had tried to turn the car. When he had seen the other driver, his main goal had been to push mine and Stephen's side into the guardrail, so he could take the full force of the collision. There had not been enough time, however. We had hit almost head on. As a father, Jeremy felt he had not protected his family.

As well as possible, we explained to Jeremy that none of this was his fault; that he had done all he could. While it would take months to truly heal emotionally, I knew Jeremy felt as I did that God had a greater plan.

Nothing we could have done that day would have changed this part of His perfect will for our family. God was working, and we knew we could trust Him.

No matter how long or short our visit that day, those moments were precious. Seeing Stephen in Jeremy's arms was a dream I had been imagining for a long time. Just having our family on the same floor of the hospital was a huge answer to prayer. I praised God for that miracle and looked ahead with excitement. Our hearts had never been separated, but our lives had been. God was mending our family.

11

Monday, September 17-Tuesday, September 18

"The righteous cry out, and the Lord hears them; he

delivers them from all their troubles. The Lord is close to

the brokenhearted and saves those who are crushed in

spirit."

-Psalm 34:17,18

Surprisingly, it was brought up early the next day

that Jeremy may possibly go home. We were all cautiously

optimistic. My constant desire had been that we all go

home together. I wasn't sure what I would do if Jeremy

went home first. Leaving Stephen seemed terrible, but I

couldn't imagine Jeremy going home by himself. I even

contemplated the idea of Jeremy moving into the Ronald

McDonald House with me. On the other hand, if Stephen

was released first, we would have to move from the Ronald

McDonald House. Policy stated that you must have a child

in the hospital to stay there. I wasn't sure where we would

move to if this happened and who, if not myself, would go home with Stephen. The only solution to this dilemma would have to be the home going of us as a family.

Excited does not began to explain how Jeremy felt about going home. He had been asking about this day for over a week. After further discussion by his doctors, Jeremy was disappointed to find out he would not be leaving the hospital yet. He was still too weak to sit up and had only begun learning to transfer to his wheelchair. At this point, it would take at least 3 men to move him. He was helpless on his own. The issue of his appetite also came into question. Jeremy's doctors feared that if he went home and continued not eating, he would end up being re-admitted in the days to come. He, like Stephen, had to get some of his appetite back before he was going anywhere.

Every day from then on we were required to keep a log of what Jeremy ate. His parents would beg him to try anything. People would bring him outside food from any restaurant he requested. If he took a bite of anything, we would write it down. Tic-Tacs were even included...We were desperate! Each morning a nurse would come by and collect this food log. Each day we would pray it had been enough food.

After Stephen's enjoyable ride to his Daddy's room the day before, his trips became more regular. Sometimes Joe and Judy or Daren and Kim would just push him around right outside his room. The hospital let them borrow a little pop-up stroller. Stephen seemed much more content getting out of his room. It was a needed change for everyone who had been taking care of him. Often when I visited in the days ahead, I would find him strolling in the waiting room. His precious smile was coming back. It reassured me he was still our sweet, little Stephen.

Those in charge of both the Pollard Update and the Care Pages had asked me if I had anything I wanted them to share with those keeping up with our progress. I had said yes, but wasn't sure where I could begin. Later that afternoon, out of nowhere, the Holy Spirit clearly gave me what to say. I called Brenda in and asked her to write. These are the first words I posted after the wreck. This is what the Holy Spirit led me to write:

"Heal the wound but leave the scar, to remind me of how merciful you are." "I am still confident of this, I will see the goodness of the Lord in the land of the living. Wait for the Lord; be strong and take heart; wait for the Lord."

On August 27, our family entered a storm and since that evening, many of you have been traveling with us. Jeremy is doing much better and hopes to go home the first of this week. Pray for strength. Stephen is daily improving, and we hope to take him home later this week. Pray for grace and for his appetite.

Thank you for all the prayers and encouraging comments. You are continually lifting my spirits. Please keep interceding for us.

"All I am and ever hope to be, I owe it all to

Thee...to God be the glory."

—Tiffany

My limited words could never truly express my thoughts during this time. No thank you could ever truly say how grateful I was to the hundreds of people who were praying. No tears could ever contain the pain that often filled my heart. No beautiful phrase could ever explain the peace that flooded my soul. No smile could portray the joy that God had given even in this Storm. No one could truly understand me but God.

It had been twenty-two days since the wreck. Time had flown so quickly yet so slowly at the same time. Each of us, including family and friends, was different. Our lives had changed.

After getting off the elevator Tuesday morning, we were greeted by Stephen in his stroller. Judy walked behind and maneuvered his little chariot here and there. He grinned as they rolled him into the play area of the hospital. I watched as he looked at all the toys and balls. As best he could, Stephen began to toss a little ball back and forth with Joe. I could hardly wait to get him home and see him playing with his toys. I imagined his little stuffed animals and cars missed him as much as he missed them.

Thoughts of home flooded my mind. I imagined our living room. I saw the kitchen. The memory of Stephen playing in his playroom seemed distant. Where had the time gone? We had left our home on August 27 with no intention of not returning. How unexpected life can be.

I even thought of our two Labrador Retrievers, Joy and Lady. They had been a part of our family since we got married. These loving dogs were our babies until Stephen came along. Somehow they too must have wondered where we were.

In total faith, many of our friends had stepped in and begun preparing our home for our arrival. I had heard that a ramp had been installed leading up to the front door. Someone even told me that a company had voluntarily concreted a semi-circle drive leading up to our front door. Jeremy and I had dreamed of this new access for years now. The volleyball team had come in and cleaned from top to bottom. Our Pastor's wife had taken direct requests from me concerning food and other things that needed to be done. I imagined what our home must now look like. From what I heard, it had been transformed into a makeshift hospital. We just wanted to go home.

As I watched Stephen play ball, I again noticed his left eye. Each time he attempted to look straight, that little eye would pull in, almost parallel to his nose. It was almost as if he had developed a severe lazy eye. I knew it had not been like this before the wreck.

Joe said that the doctors knew about Stephen's eye, but that nothing had been done. They were so concerned with the healing of his neck and his appetite that this issue had been overlooked. My Mom pushed me back to Stephen's room, and I spoke to his nurse. With Stephen eating more now, I hoped he would go home soon. His eye needed to be checked while he was still in the hospital.

Later that afternoon, Stephen was taken down to the eye center of the hospital. Joe sat in a wheelchair and held Stephen, as a nurse pushed them to another floor. I watched them roll away and wished I could go with them. Joe would take care of Stephen, but I desperately wanted to meet with this Dr. also.

As we waited, I prayed this was nothing serious. Stephen's doctor had mentioned that this could be related to his neck injury; that he could have slight brain damage that would be affecting his eye. The neck surgery had been successful but with injuries like this, you never know. Please, Lord, protect Stephen. Let this be minor. He's suffered enough.

Joe and Stephen returned within an hour and reported what the eye doctor had found. In addition to the neck injury Stephen had, the nerves in his left eye had also been damaged. Both Stephen's 4th and 6th nerves were affected, which left his eye unable to remain straight. While curious as to the remedy, I praised God that it was nothing more serious.

A little black eye patch was put into my hand. For the next several months, Stephen would have to wear this patch 2-3 hours a day. We would place it on his good eye each morning, so his weak eye would be forced to work. If we didn't make the damaged eye work, however, it would begin to shut down and Stephen would permanently lose vision in that eye. A follow-up visit had been scheduled, and we all prayed Stephen would adjust well to this patch and keep his vision.

Later that same day, Jeremy had his normal physical therapy session. He had even felt comfortable enough in the wheelchair to visit Stephen's room. Every one could see the progress he was making.

That evening we spent several hours talking and sharing our hearts. The Holy Spirit prompted me, and I knew it was time to share with Jeremy about the baby we had lost. People were anxious and wanting to know if I was still pregnant. I had avoided the question until I had a chance to talk to Jeremy. It would have been devastating for him to find out through someone else.

I took his hand in mine, and tears began to spill over onto my cheeks. I didn't know where to start. With all that Jeremy had already been digesting, I almost felt guilty putting something else on his plate. How do you tell a father his child is gone? I put my fears aside and began. It was time.

Jeremy looked at me as I quietly said, "Jeremy, God took the baby we were carrying." It was all I could say. My throat closed up, and the tears came uncontrollably. Jeremy looked at me with more peace and compassion than I have ever seen and responded, "I know."

I was so surprised but could not get out the word "how?". In answer to this unasked question Jeremy responded, "I just knew." In the days ahead our compassionate God had already prepared Jeremy for this moment. Jeremy knew, before I spoke a word, that our child was now in Heaven. He had been waiting for me to bring it up. God was still on His throne and working. He had told Jeremy about the baby in a more perfect way than I ever could have. He had spoken directly to Jeremy's heart. What I could not do, the Holy Spirit had already taken care of. That's the loving God we serve.

Later that night I again released a statement to those who had been praying. There would be no more awkward, "Are you still pregnant questions?". I knew people would begin bathing this in prayer as they had all the other storms our family was facing. The emotional healing from the miscarriage had begun. The following statement was Holy Spirit breathed:

"The Lord gave and the Lord has taken away; may the name of the Lord be praised." (Job 1:21b)

In His infinite wisdom, God has chosen to take our unborn child. He knows how difficult it would be for me to take care of my recovering family and be pregnant at the same time. Jeremy and I are at peace knowing that if God had to take one of us, He chose this one. We are already so blessed! Please continue keeping our family in your prayers.

-Tiffany

12

Wednesday, September 19

"Do you not know? Have you not heard? The Lord is the everlasting God, the Creator of the ends of the earth. He will not grow tired or weary, and his understanding no one can fathom. He gives strength to the weary and increases the power of the weak. Even youths grow tired and weary and young men stumble and fall; but those who hope in the Lord will renew their strength. They will soar on wings like eagles; they will run and not grow weary, they will walk and not be faint."

-Isaiah 40:28-31

What disbelief filled my heart the next morning when I visited Stephen's room! I could tell by the smiles and Joe and Judy's faces that something big had happened. Just minutes before, Stephen's nurse had come in and removed the feeding tube. In the next few hours, Stephen would be going home!

I could not contain the overwhelming joy that flooded my soul. Everyone in the room that morning cried. My baby, our son who had fought and barely survived, was now strong enough to go home! Thank You, thank You, thank You, fled my lips to Heaven! The day had started off so beautifully!

With this exciting news came many plans. Who would go home with Stephen? Where would he stay this first night? We only had a couple of hours to get things arranged.

Knowing Jeremy was also very close to going home, I decided to stay near the hospital. We contacted the Ronald McDonald House and were relieved to find out parents have 24 hours to check out once their child has been released. I could stay one last night there but would have to leave tomorrow. What a miracle if Jeremy could go home by then! That way, no other arrangements would have to be made.

My Mom was willing to go home with Stephen, but I still needed her with me. Joe and Judy graciously volunteered to drive Stephen home. That night, Daren and Kim would stay at our house with Stephen. They would continue their regular routine, just at home instead of the hospital. We are so blessed with good friends!

Jeremy had to know about Stephen! While we waited for all the paperwork to be completed, my Mom pushed me to visit Jeremy. I found him in the hallway sitting in his wheelchair. He was finishing up physical therapy and wanted to remain out of bed a little longer. Each day he was looking stronger.

He was as excited as I was about Stephen's home going. Now, more than ever, he also wanted to go home. I told him about having to check-out of the Ronald McDonald House the following day, and we prayed maybe he could leave by then. If not, we would play it by ear.

Jeremy's therapist came by to help him get back into his hospital bed, so I returned to Stephen's room. Not long after returning, one of Stephen's doctors came in carrying a stack of papers. This was it! A couple last minute instructions, some signatures, and Stephen was free to leave!

"Are you serious?" I asked him. "He can really go home?" This young doctor smiled and reassured me that yes, our son was free to leave! I signed the papers as best I could while Stephen's last few personal items were gathered up. For the first time in weeks, I saw him in regular clothes! That blue and white hospital gown was a thing of the past! In the months ahead I would hold that little gown and weep tears of joy. God had brought us so far! He is so faithful!

Mom pushed my wheelchair out the hospital room door toward the elevator. Joe and Judy walked ahead of us with Stephen in Joe's arms. I never wanted to return to this place. I kissed our squirmy, little boy on the head as the elevator door closed. Stephen was on his way home!

That same exciting day, Jeremy gave his first statement to the Pollard Update. Due to his condition, I had been our family's spokesman for weeks now. I gladly handed Jeremy back the reigns. He could assume his duties as head of the family. These are the words he shared...

"Trust in the Lord with all your heart and lean not on your own understanding; in all your ways submit to him, and he will make your paths straight." (Proverbs 3:5,6)

Dear Friends in Christ,

The last 3 and a half weeks have been, by far, the toughest in my life. But one of the great things about these verses is that God gives two distinct commands-one, to trust and two, to submit to Him in everything.

If there is one thing that my family and I have learned it is that trusting God is not the easiest thing to do, but when we lean on Him, even in rough times like this, His promise is true and He will direct our paths.

I would like to thank each of you for the many thousands of prayers you have lifted up on behalf of my family. We are all improving and looking forward to being together at home soon.

When your storm comes, I hope that each of you will do as our families have done. Be faithful to pray and trust HIM in the storm.

Hoping to see my Union Grove church family in a few weeks,

Jeremy Pollard

Student Pastor

After several hours of Stephen being back home, Joe called with an update on how things were going. As soon as Stephen had entered the door, he seemed calmer and more like himself. Judy had carried him over to the miniature basketball goal we had bought just days before

the wreck. Stephen took a ball and from Judy's arms, shot
it right in the goal! Jeremy and I felt much more peace
knowing Stephen was no longer in the hospital. At least
one of us was home!

The evening was spent in Jeremy's room. He was
eating a little more and hopeful on going home the
following day. His social worker came by, and we made
sure everything Jeremy would need at home had been
ordered. This included his wheelchair, sliding board, and a
rented hospital bed. Everything was on its way, and the
hospital bed would be delivered to our home the following
day.

Pastor and Kim came over again, and we made sure
everything at home was ready if need be. I would sleep in a
twin bed pushed up beside Jeremy's hospital bed. After
measuring our doorways, someone had realized that the
wheelchairs would not fit into the bedroom. Our beds
would be set up in the living room. Shower curtains would

be hung to provide makeshift walls as our home is very open. Whoever stayed with us each night could sleep in our bedroom. Whoever stayed with Stephen could sleep upstairs in the extra bedroom next to his nursery.

As desperately as Jeremy and I wanted to go home, we were a little nervous. This would be a huge adjustment. All 3 of us needed a lot of help. God had gotten us this far, and He would not leave us now. For tonight, we would sleep and wait to see what tomorrow held.

13

Thursday, September 20

"In his heart a man plans his course, but the Lord

determines his steps."

-Proverbs 16:9

After little sleep for everyone, Thursday came.

Today I would be leaving the Ronald McDonald House. No

one knew yet if I would be going home or to a local motel.

Brenda stayed behind to pack up our bags while Mom took

me over to visit Jeremy.

He had not yet heard from his doctor. His physical

therapy had already been done, and his Mom reported that

Jeremy had done well. Although still needing a lot of help,

his therapist believed he was ready to go home. Jeremy's

family was willing to do whatever they needed to.

The only hold back was again Jeremy's appetite.

His food log had looked better the past couple days but still

not what it needed to be. Jeremy's primary doctor was out

today. We all feared he would have to wait another day until this doctor returned. We were discouraged but holding on to hope. The Lord's timing was best.

Kim called to let us know how Stephen had done his first night at home. She said he had slept a little better but not great. He still cried a lot. A small bed had been placed in Stephen's room beside his crib. Kim slept there, and Stephen slept beside her. As an infant, I had always insisted Stephen sleep in his own bed. He had slept in a pack and play in our room for the first 5 months of his life. After that he had been sleeping upstairs. Now, though, all my rules didn't seem so important. Stephen just needed his sleep, and Jeremy and I would have to be flexible.

The doctor covering in Jeremy's doctor's absence came in to introduce himself to us. After looking over Jeremy's paperwork, he felt ready to make a decision on Jeremy's going home. We would not have to wait another day. This doctor had made the decision. He did not think

that Jeremy needed to stay another night in that hospital!
Jeremy was ready to go home!

A flood of happiness again filled our hearts! We
could hardly believe it! Despite our fears and questions,
God was healing us. Jeremy was excited and ready to go
right then! Unfortunately, his paperwork still had to be
completed. Like Stephen, there were also arrangements to
be made. Who would transport us?

It was quickly decided that I could ride in my
parent's SUV while Jeremy would ride in one of the
hospital vans that I had been using so often. A man in our
church who worked for the hospital made the
arrangements. This would make things so much easier for
Jeremy. He was unable to bend either of his legs and could
not possibly fit in a regular vehicle. I worried a little about
his motion sickness as his wheelchair would be placed in
the back of the van. Surely he could make it the short 15

minutes to our house. Maybe his adrenaline would take over!

Mom and I went back over to the Ronald McDonald House to make sure everything had been packed and was ready to go. We also said farewell to several of the women who had made us feel at home the past two weeks. The car was loaded, and we headed back over to the hospital to wait with Jeremy.

Soon after we returned, Jeremy's hospital phone rang. His Mom answered and immediately handed the phone to Jeremy. A look of confusion swept his face as he said, "Yes, that should be fine." From there, I attempted to guess at who he was talking to. When he said we would call them back later, I was even more confused. Who could be so important as to need a call back on this very special day?

Jeremy hung up, and my questions were quickly answered. A reporter from the local news station that had been covering our story was the party on the other line. They had gotten word we were going home. Per our acceptance, they wanted to cover our going home live. Jeremy, knowing I would agree, had said yes. A news crew was presently on the way to our home. They would set up and wait for us to call when we got close. Jeremy gave me the reporter's number. I would hopefully be calling her back soon.

As afternoon came we began to get a little impatient. Everything was packed and we were ready to go. Jeremy's hospital room was empty again. The walls were bare. He sat on the bed without the TV even on. The silence and expectation were almost deafening.

Finally, I decided to take action. It had been too long. Surely, Jeremy's paperwork was ready by now. My Dad pushed me outside Jeremy's room to the nurses' station. I politely asked them when Jeremy Pollard could go home and how much longer it would be until his paperwork was completed. The nurse looked around her desk and up to a stack of papers sitting on the edge. "Here they are," she said, "He's ready to go."

Jeremy was more than surprised when my wheelchair came into the door with a nurse following behind. He was even more shocked to see that she held the paperwork we had been waiting for. After a few quick guidelines and signatures, Jeremy was ready to go home!

It was a huge deal getting all the vehicles pulled around and ready to pick us up. With our families, we made a huge (and excited) caravan. Some final adjustments were made to Jeremy's wheelchair, and we were ready to leave.

Jeremy and I were pushed side by side through the 11th floor of the hospital. I waved goodbye as we passed the small room where I had stayed. The nurses said farewell; some with tears in their eyes. They had become very dear to us. As much as we wanted to leave, we would miss some of the friendships we had made. God had united us in a way only He could.

We sat side by side on the small elevator. There was barely enough room for all of us. My Dad pushed the G for Ground Floor, and the elevator began traveling down. The door soon reopened, and we headed toward the exit. I could see the sun shining as we neared the parking lot.

Being outside of the hospital with Jeremy was almost unbelievable. The hustle of our continued busy world seemed to overwhelm him as it had done me before. Jeremy had not felt the wind on his face in almost four weeks. He had lived in the bubble of that large hospital. Life for most others, however, had not stopped.

Our wheelchairs were pushed over to the side where we could load without interrupting the flow of traffic. Jeremy was pushed on the ramp of a hospital van. The driver, whom I knew from past trips, strapped him down and raised the small platform even with the back doors.

Jeremy was then rolled off the ramp and strapped into the back of the van.

Two hospital employees had been deciding on the best course for loading me while I had been watching Jeremy. As carefully as possible, they lifted me from the wheelchair and placed me sideways in the back of my parent's SUV. My wheelchair was quickly folded and placed in the trunk. I hoped we would remember how to open it back up. I also prayed our family would be able to move me as painlessly as the two trained men had just done.

Both vans pulled out of the parking lot and headed towards our home. Not a block from the hospital, the van carrying Jeremy pulled over in front of us. I feared he was already getting motion sick. His driver got out and headed to the back. My Mom had been riding with Jeremy, and I tried to gather clues as I watched her face through the van's back window. Thankfully the driver told my Dad that

Jeremy's wheelchair had been shifting a little. He had not been strapped in as tightly as needed. Everything was now okay, and we headed back into traffic.

As both vehicles stopped at lights and made their way toward home, my mind was flooded with memories. This trip was the first one both Jeremy and I had made in a normal vehicle since August 27. I had sworn to myself I would never ride in the front seat of a small car again. The large SUV gave me a limited sense of safety.

Vehicles passed us on the right and left. How carelessly we often drive. Our lives, our understanding of the responsibility of driving had changed. We would forever be more careful; often to the point of fearful. A couple more turns, and we were on the road where the wreck had taken place.

I began to think about Stephen waiting on us at home. Seeing him back in his normal environment seemed almost a dream. There had been days where I truly thought

I would have made this trip home by myself. Jeremy and Stephen's improvement had been miracles. We were going home as a family...no packing boxes of toys...no deciding what to do with Jeremy's clothes...no removing family pictures from our walls. My fears had been wiped away by the gracious hand of our loving Father. He was giving our life back!

Remembering Jeremy's conversation with the news station, I began to dial the reporter's number. We were about 6 miles from the house. They were already there and waiting.

Since our wreck had taken place on a main road, there was really no alternate route to take to get home. We would soon be passing the site where our lives had been changed. Any time we left in the days ahead, we would drive by this sight. It was time to go ahead and face it. I had wondered for hours how both Jeremy and I would respond as we drove past.

The closer we got, the quicker the tears began to fall. I could hardly tell what emotion was causing them. Was it joy that we were going home? Was it anger at what had taken place? Was it sorrow over what our family had gone through? I was overwhelmed.

As we drove around the curve, I could see the spot where our two vehicles had collided. I thought about closing my eyes but somehow couldn't. My body forced me to look; to remember. A small patch of sand still lay where our car had stopped that night. The sounds and smells all came rushing back. For months, the memories would flood Jeremy's and my mind each time we drove past this spot. We would relive that unexpected night. We would thank God for His provision and presence.

While overtaken with emotion, my heart was grateful. There could be memorial flowers in that spot. I had seen this type of flower many times on the side of the road. Who would have ever dreamed we were that close to having them placed in our memory? My heart placed a small bouquet beside the pile of sand in honor of the baby God had taken. We had given up something in that wreck. But by God's goodness, we would see our child again.

No sooner had we come up on the scene than we were past it and pulling onto the road where we lived. As we neared our driveway, a huge TV antenna came into view. The cameras were ready and already rolling. My mind could hardly take in all that I saw and everything that happened in the next few moments.

A large sign had been placed in our yard. It read "Welcome Home." Balloons were attached to it and swaying in the wind. They read "With God all things are possible." In the front yard stood so many people. Several of them were holding handmade signs.

We followed the van Jeremy rode in as it pulled down the neighbor's driveway. This driveway ran parallel to our front door. We had always wanted to attach our own driveway, so visitors would have easy access to our home. I was shocked as both vehicles pulled onto the newly paved semi-circle drive that had been completed while we were in the hospital. It was what Jeremy and I had always wanted for our home! We could not have done it better ourselves!

The van and SUV easily pulled us up to our front door. Jeremy was again placed on the van's platform and lowered to the ground. The news cameras were immediately beside him with the reporter asking him questions. A couple men carefully removed me from the backseat and placed me back into the wheelchair. Dad pushed me up beside Jeremy and I grabbed his hand. We sat in front our home…together! It was a miracle moment only God could have done.

Both of us answered a couple more questions for the news station. Those gathered there that day clapped as we were pushed toward the front door. Both family and friends were there. The entire soccer team stood and watched their assistant coach. They too had suffered. So many of these precious people had prayed. They had been waiting for this moment as long as we had.

Joe held Stephen on the front porch. As we rolled up the newly made wheelchair ramp, I kissed him hello. Yes, my dear baby, Daddy and Mommy are now home! This day, these moments were some of the most precious of our lives!

Once inside our home Jeremy and I were amazed at all the work that had been done. The new driveway and ramps had only been the beginning. We were both exhausted and desperately wanted to get out of those wheelchairs and in the bed. Both of us kept saying, however, "Look at that…Can you believe they did that?" It was almost like a home makeover but one creating a hospital out of a normal home.

Large bottles of hand sanitizer sat everywhere. It was very important to keep germs out as all three of us had weak immune systems. Our toddler stained carpet had even been cleaned. New sheets lay on both beds and beckoned Jeremy and I to rest. For the first time on their own, our families moved each of us from wheelchair to bed. Those practice times with the therapist in the hospital had really paid off. The transitions went amazingly smooth and pain free. Both Jeremy and I had feared not having the help of professional medical care. The days ahead would teach us to rely even more on our families. Often love can do a better job than training.

That first night at home brought adjustments for everyone. Within minutes of getting into our beds, someone reminded us that the news was about to come on. The TV was turned on, and everyone gathered around our beds in the living room. Our images on the screen were almost shocking.

For the first time, Jeremy realized how weak and sick he looked. His thin body and pale skin reminded all of us how close death had been. The weeks in a coma had taken their toll. It would take months for him to look more like his old self.

My appearance was more similar to my normal self. The two weeks in the Ronald McDonald House had done me good. While still very weak, it was easily detectable that I was improving. Emotionally, though, viewers knew I was on overload. The tears never stopped.

Stephen's precious little face is the one that will forever fill the hearts of many who saw the newscast that night. Over and over they showed his little face, scrunched up in his neck brace. His left eye pulled in as he innocently looked at the news camera. Close-ups of him covered the screen time and time again during the interview. He, like his parents, had been through a storm. But oh, how faithful God had been. Stephen was a living testament to God's unbelievable grace.

The news story was one of hope and healing. The reporter, a Christian lady, clearly shared how God had done this miracle in our lives. She would later set up a blog where we could more easily share the Gospel with those interested in our story. In the future, this same station would continue covering our family's journey as we met different milestones. Jeremy and I still laugh as we remember the time they reported that Jeremy had gotten one of his casts off. Everyone was pulling for us!

Ladies from the church again brought us supper that night. They had not stopped since two weeks ago and would continue through December. These meals always tasted great and helped us get our appetites back. This sacrifice took a huge burden off our families.

Plans were made as to how we would handle this first night. Someone would stay in the upstairs bedroom near Stephen's room. Another person would sleep in our bed as to be near to the living room where Jeremy and I slept. Each of us would need almost 24 hour care.

The news cast aired again later that night. As we watched Stephen's sweet face on the television screen, both Jeremy and I realized something. Our prayer that God use Stephen "now and later" was already being answered. Here he was, a 17-month old, proclaiming to thousands of viewers around the area that God is good; that we serve a miracle working Father! And to think that Stephen hadn't even said a word! Yes, God *was* using him!

The next few days, weeks, and even months held more than anyone could ever write. There were good days and, of course, there were very trying days. Some days Jeremy and I would smile at God's goodness. Other days we would question all we had been through. There were still so many pieces to put together.

Many nights we would lay awake until the early morning hours. Our hearts would break as Stephen's cries filled our ears from his room upstairs. Visitors would come in and out. Letters flooded the mailbox. Meetings with physical therapists often brought pain and frustration. We were still in a storm.

But through it all, each trial and triumphant, God was good. He was working in our hearts in ways we can barely describe. Each day, August 27, 2007 and all those from then until now had not changed the truth of God's Word. His plans are always best and He will see us through what He calls us to. God is a loving Father, and He can be trusted. We could never doubt the love God showed us on Calvary. He is working even in life's darkest moments. He is weaving a beautiful tapestry for each of us; for every family. Even on the tough days, even when the questions still linger, we can choose to say, "This is the day that the Lord has made; we will rejoice and be glad in it."

A Final Word

"But what can I say? He has spoken to me, and he himself

has done this. I will walk humbly all my years because of

this anguish of my soul. Lord, by such things men live; and

my spirit finds life in them too. You restored me to health

and let me live. Surely it was for my benefit that I suffered

such anguish. In your love you kept me from the pit of

destruction; you have put all my sins behind your back. For

the grave cannot praise you, death cannot sing your praise;

those who go down to the pit cannot hope for your

faithfulness. The living, the living-they praise you, as I am

doing today; father tells their children about your

faithfulness."

-Isaiah 38:15-19

As much as our storm ended with our homegoing, it

was really only the beginning. For months, we adapted to a

new way of life. Friends and family continued putting their

lives on hold. Jeremy, Stephen, and I were completely

reliant on others. We could do nothing for ourselves.

Stephen was a 17 month old in the body of an

infant. He could not sit up, crawl, or walk. Someone had to

constantly hold him or push him in the stroller. At

Stephen's first follow-up with the neurosurgeon, we were

all relieved at the doctor's positive prognosis. His x-rays

showed that Stephen had healed enough to no longer need

to wear the neck brace 24 hours a day. We would only have

to put it on him in the car. It had only been six weeks since

his surgery, and we were originally told he would have to

wear it for at least twelve. We were thrilled!

For a couple weeks after that appointment, Stephen

could not hold his head up. His chin rested on his chest.

The muscles in his neck had become weak from disuse. We

prayed he would regain strength quickly and would do

things to encourage this, such as holding toys slightly

above eye level. A physical therapist came in and worked

with him some. Within weeks, we saw noticeable improvement. His bandages were removed, and the redness began to fade. The shaved portion of his hair began to grow back as fuzz. Minus the scars, he was beginning to look like our little boy again…"fearfully and wonderfully made."

At another follow-up appointment an MRI had to be done on Stephen's neck. This meant he had to lie completely still. My Mom and I took him to the hospital. They gave him a liquid to drink and put us in a dark, quiet room. For about an hour Mom walked him. I tried to rock him some. He finally fell asleep. During the MRI, I waited in the little room and prayed he was continuing to heal well. A poster on the wall spoke to me that day, and I have carried the quote with me since. It read, "The will of God won't lead you where the grace of God won't keep you." The MRI came back well, and Stephen was healing wonderfully.

Our last visit to the neurosurgeon was a relief. We were thrilled when they released him. From now on, we will have to continue taking him one time each year for a check-up. The x-rays we've seen are amazing. Stephen's Dr. watched him in awe as he ran all over the room. He commented that Stephen already had more than the 50% neck movement they thought he would have. Besides avoiding sports such as football and hockey, Stephen can do about anything he wants. Unless he grows to be over six foot tall (which is completely unlikely to happen), his body will grow around the plate and screws, and he will not require another surgery. Stephen's Doctor and we were very pleased.

For months, we continued visits to the eye doctor. Stephen would wear his little patch several hours each morning. Sometimes he would fuss, but he never messed with it. When we would go out, people would look at him so curiously. Occasionally they were brave enough to ask what happened, and I would tell them about the wreck.

Sometimes, I would just tell them he wanted to be a pirate!

Stephen acquired some pretty cute nicknames.

He had a Botox injection once on the nerves in his

left eye. It was an outpatient surgery at 6 am. Jeremy had

also had his second army surgery the week before.

Needless to say, those were crazy times in our lives. The

nurse put a little blue x above Stephen's eye to mark which

one he would have surgery on. We washed and washed, but

the marker stained his face for weeks. It's in some of our

Christmas pictures! The medicine they gave him as

sedation worked perfectly. He was a cute, drunk 20 month

old! This first injection was successful but didn't provide

complete healing. Upon moving to Durham, we were

referred to another eye Dr. who did surgery on Stephen's

eyes. They have greatly improved, and presently the only

repercussions require him to wear reading glass and dark

tinted sunglasses outside.

One day, in addition to the cards we received, Stephen received a special package. It was a CD from the organization Songs of Love. This company creates personalized songs for kids who are suffering from all kinds of different health issues. They do this free of charge. I had forgotten I had filled out a form for Stephen to get one of these CD's during my stay at the Ronald McDonald House. When we first played it, it was absolutely perfect. It included so many things that reminded us of the Stephen before and the Stephen we hoped to see again. The CD was almost played out, and we will cherish it forever.

When we first got home and began living on our own as a normal family again, Stephen struggled with some separation anxiety. His pediatrician said it was completely normal, especially considering what he'd been through. In one quick moment, both his Daddy and Mommy were taken away from him. One can only imagine the confusion in his little mind. Taking him to our church's nursery was often an impossibility. He would usually ask, "Mama come back and get me?" I tried to reassure him that "Yes, Lord willing, Mama *will* come back and get him." Most of the time I just ended up staying with him. Now that I could comfort him, it tore me apart to hear him cry when I knew I could stop it. For weeks, I heard him scream and could do nothing to comfort him.

Jeremy and I would lay in our beds in the living room and do our best to ignore the cries coming from upstairs. My Mom would close Stephen's bedroom door in an attempt to muffle the sound. As a mother, you learn to hear your child's cry. It was hard to pretend I didn't hear it. We have concluded that next to losing your child, hearing your child suffer and not being able to help him must be the hardest thing a parent has to go through. I imagine that's a touch of how God felt watching His Son on the cross. Knowing He could help but refusing to do so because of His love for us. That mercy and grace is mind-boggling.

One particular evening, Jeremy and I could take the crying no more. It was hard watching our parents raise our son. Jeremy could not be the head of the house, and I could not be the wife I had always been. Our roles were gone. Our jobs as parents were not able to be ours for those months. Jeremy's parents pushed our wheelchairs outside, and alone in the darkness Jeremy and I wept. We agreed we could not be Stephen's parents right now. We had to hand the reins over to our parents and trust God to lead them. It was hard letting go. We prayed and headed back into the house with a new perspective.

Stephen continues to be our little miracle boy. He is so sweet-natured and tender hearted. No one would even know he had been in the wreck if they weren't told, or they didn't notice his scars. Jeremy and I have shared with our son what God did in his and our lives through the wreck. We have shown him the newspapers clippings. We have prayed with Him and cried anew at God's provision. We remind Stephen that God had a purpose then and has a purpose now for his life.

Blessed does not begin to explain how we feel when it comes to Stephen. We treasure every day, every little milestone. I cry at the little things I am able to do with him. Jeremy and I see things in a different light. God has given a tremendous responsibility in the life of our son. Our desire is to bring glory to Him. We could never say "Thank You Father" enough.

Jeremy has healed very well. He was able to walk much sooner than the doctors expected. His arm gave him trouble for months, and he ended up having three surgeries on it. The nerve damage has affected his movement and feeling in his pinky. Between therapy, wearing crazy arm braces, and the TLC I try to give it at home, we have seen him get most of his motion and strength back.

For months, Jeremy ached to play golf. On warm days, he wished he was out on some beautiful golf course.

The lack of grip in his hand made this impossible. After some thought, Jeremy got each of his golf clubs re-gripped. The larger grip would make it easier for him to hold on to the clubs, especially with his injured left hand. On June 18, Jeremy played his first complete 18 holes of golf. He (and all of us who knew how much this meant to him) was ecstatic. He shot an 87, which was definitely better than he thought he would do. It had been about 10 months since his last round. He bought Stephen his first real set of clubs and has recently enjoyed a few rounds with him.

Jeremy returned to work at church in December. Pastor and the other leaders had done an incredible job at taking care of things in his absence. He adjusted well and thoroughly enjoyed being back at work.

Someone stood in for Jeremy as basketball coach until he could return. Jeremy coached his first game on a walker. He was determined to get back out there. He loved and missed the guys. Jeremy was able to briefly share our testimony at a tournament, and we were given a standing ovation. So many people had been praying for us.

We returned to church on a Sunday night in October. As our parents pushed our wheelchairs through the center aisle, again the people stood up and clapped. They were so grateful to see us back. Both Jeremy and I shared briefly with the church that night and thanked them for everything they had done. It was a very emotional service for all of us.

Later in October we returned to the youth group. It was a special evangelistic night that Jeremy had planned long before the wreck. A guest speaker and ensemble were there to sing. The night was termed "STORM" even before we knew of the storm our family would go through. Over 150 students were there that night! 22 of these students accepted Christ as their Savior! Jeremy and I were in awe! It was amazing being back with the students and leaders we had missed so much.

The news station was again there for this big youth night. They interviewed me, Jeremy, and some of the students. One of the camera guys commented to us that it wasn't every day they met nice people like us. We were just surprised they were there. Along with that night at the Grove, they also aired a story on a benefit motorcycle ride that was done for us. To conclude their coverage, the three of us did a live interview early one morning. We were able to announce to them and the hundreds of viewers watching that we were expecting again! Everyone in the studio clapped. It was neat being there but admittedly a little stressful. Stephen was back to his normal, busy self! Everyone said this was good to see though!

Even though years have passed, we still think of our Heaven baby. I weep each year on the due date. It seems like a piece of our family is still missing. Admittedly, I struggled deeply with losing that baby. With Jeremy and Stephen demanding so much of my emotions in the hospital, I had not had a chance to fully comprehend and deal with the miscarriage we had experienced. Often (and expectedly) people were so curious about how the three of us were doing that the baby got forgotten. In my soul, though, I was hurting.

At my last follow-up with the ob-gyn my blood level finally showed zero. I had gone for a check-up while at the Ronald McDonald House and another after we came home. Each time my hormone level was still a little elevated, and they discussed doing a D&C. We all prayed things would go back to normal, so this additional procedure could be avoided. Each time I visited this doctor, I ached. The waiting room was always filled with expecting mothers. Here I sat in a wheelchair. I always felt like all eyes were on me, while I tried to keep a smile. At this visit, I felt so much relief yet so much pain. Jeremy had not been able to go; we were obviously still weak and healing. When my Aunt Brenda and I returned home, she pushed me in our bedroom. Per my request, she shut the door, and I sobbed for the child I longed to hold. Was I grateful to still have Jeremy and Stephen? Of course, but I realized we had lost something.

For months and months, I continued to heal. I would see other pregnant women and feel jealously rising in my throat. When babies were due close to our baby's due date, I would hurt even more. Finally, it was time for me to deal with this. Jeremy and Stephen were better, and in my quiet time, I began to read books on dealing with a miscarriage.

Through these quiet moments, prayer, and the working of the Holy Spirit, I slowly healed. I realize that one day I will hold this child again. I understand that he or she is right now experiencing more joy than Jeremy and I could have ever given. Each day, I long for Heaven a little more.

Before we could try to get pregnant again, three

different doctors had to give us their approval: my ob-gyn

due to the miscarriage, my internal doctor due to the torn

intestine, and my orthopedic doctor due to the increased

weight that would be put on my healing bones. Finally, we

got three yeses and the anticipation begun.

Both Stephen and our Heaven baby were conceived

in three months. We were expecting the same for our next

child. After one month, I was late. Jeremy and I could only

dream that we were pregnant this fast. We took a

pregnancy test and were disappointed when the "not

pregnant" flashed on the screen. For a little over three

months, we got the same results. I couldn't understand

God's purpose in making us wait. We had endured so much

"for Him." Surely, He wanted to give us another child.

In fear, Jeremy and I scheduled another

appointment with my ob-gyn. I imagined that something

with my internal injuries was affecting our ability to

conceive. The doctor assured us that everything looked okay but that due to the physical and emotional stress my body had endured, it may take awhile.

On February 15, the day after Valentine's Day, Jeremy and I saw that positive sign we had been waiting for. To say we were excited is an understatement! We had just bought a new car two days before. Both of us secretly feared a scenario playing out as it did back in August. Thankfully, God protected us.

We strapped Stephen's infant car seat into our new car and drove around showing our friends and family the automobile we had just bought. When they opened the back door and saw two car seats, they realized what we were telling them! Since that day, we have praised God and rejoiced in His timing.

Caleb Joshua was born on October 28, 2008. He was 4 days late and has kept us in suspense since his birth. There is never a dull moment with that little guy. And he has a laugh that will make you cackle! We named him Caleb Joshua, because our prayer is that he, like the spies Joshua and Caleb in the Bible, will always see God. Even when circumstances look big and out of control, we pray Caleb will have hope. We pray He will know God is bigger than any storm that comes his way. He is a special part of our family and brings us so much joy. The Lord has been faithful. His timing, though often slower than our human minds would like, is always perfect.

To our surprise, God blessed us with another little boy on August 30, 2010. Jonathan Seth was actually due on August 27, the 3 year anniversary of the wreck. We were shocked when they told us the date. I'm convinced God has a sense of humor. Jonathan came 3 days late. He is absolutely precious and can melt the heart of anyone he meets. He looks just like his Daddy. It's hard to believe how good God has been to us. Three little boys…and we are in the process of adopting another child. I could never have dreamed up all the goodness God had in store. His ways are so perfect.

Jeremy and I were amazed at the speaking opportunities God opened up to us. We had a DVD made, which explains with pictures what God brought us through. Both of us have shared at numerous churches and special events. Jeremy had the opportunity to speak to over a hundred students at a public school Baccalaureate. In another church service, a lady came to know Christ as her Savior. We cannot begin to understand why God has chosen to use us. Our prayer is that we will continue to stay open to His leading and will for our lives. May we ever be His committed and obedient servants.

Many people have asked us how the other driver is doing. It has been our privilege to meet both this young boy and his family. At a follow-up doctor's appointment, I recognized his parents from our meeting in the hospital. I then realized that their young son was sitting beside them in a wheelchair like myself. My Mom pushed me up beside him, and I introduced myself.

I can't think of a time in my life when I have been so overwhelmed by God's love than at that moment. It was like I was seeing a family member I had been missing for years. Our lives had been so intricately inter-woven. We shared a bond no one else could understand. Only he had truly gone through what we had. He had sat in his vehicle and waited for help as our family had. He, in his own way, understood.

We talked for awhile until he was called back to see the doctor. I could have gotten out of my wheelchair and given him mercy's most comforting hug. Before he left, his Mom gave me his phone number. This was the beginning of a special relationship.

After weeks and much prayer, I called him. Since Jeremy had not yet met him, we decided it would be best if I called that first time. I played the song "Love Them Like

Jesus" over and over before I dialed his number. My prayer was that he would see Christ's love in me. We talked for awhile and at the end of the conversation, he stunned me by apologizing. He explained how he didn't know what had made him cross the center line.

I explained as best as possible that we held no hard feelings toward him; that I accepted his apology but did not need to. We knew he had not caused the wreck on purpose. Besides, if he had, it would have still been God's will. I told him that God had a greater plan for August 27 than we could ever understand. And he was a part of that plan.

In December, Jeremy, Stephen, and I visited this young boy at his home and took him a Christmas gift. This was the first time he had met Jeremy and Stephen. He apologized to Jeremy. We explained to him again how God had a purpose in all of this. As we left, we shared how God had given us a love for him that we could never understand. Jeremy often says when he speaks that you can't understand this love unless you understand the love God had for us when He sent His Son.

As we left that night, we made ourselves available to him as he healed physically and emotionally as we were doing. Jeremy and I didn't want to make him uncomfortable. He could call when he wanted to. Since then, we have spoken several times. Nearly every night at bedtime our family prays for him. Our heart's desire is that God will work in his life as He continues to do in ours.

Each member of our family continued physical therapy when we came home. All 3 of us shared the same therapist, and he would work with us at one setting. Stephen had a few sessions where he was challenged to move his neck different directions. He usually cried a lot and was definitely not making much progress. The physical therapist then gave the reigns to us. Since then we have made up and continue to use silly games to make Stephen look around. If Jeremy turns his head side to side really

quickly, Stephen tries to do the same. If we point at
something in the sky, Stephen tries to look up. He really
has made progress, and we are thankful for every bit of
mobility he has gotten back. Sometimes you have to accept
little progress before big. We saw every movement as a gift
from God.

Jeremy's and my therapy visits were sometimes the
same. We would often compete as we lay on our beds
beside each other. Needless to say, it was easier for me
being I had recovered quicker and had one fewer cast. We
would do our assigned exercises each day in an attempt to
improve. There were times when therapy really hurt as our
weak bodies were put to the test.

The first time each of us stood up was incredible. It
had been about 8 weeks. I was able to walk first and
Jeremy a couple of weeks later. As my feet touched the
floor, and my legs began to support myself, the blood
rushed and made me light-headed. I could only stand up for

a few seconds and then I had to sit down and rest. Jeremy endured the same feelings. We both wore a foot boot and used a walker for many, many weeks. The longer we practiced, the stronger we got. Before we realized it, the walkers were gone, and we were on our own. It was so exciting!

Near December, about the time we were able to walk again, our families moved out. They were a little apprehensive, but we were ready to give it a try. We put Stephen's pack-n-play up in our closet, so we didn't have to go up and down the steps to his bedroom. This lasted one night, and we realized how desperately he needed to be in his bed. We moved him back upstairs. That first night, it took both of us to walk him up the steps. Jeremy and I could barely make it up ourselves. Admittedly, it was kind of funny. Stephen slept well that first night. He only woke up once, which was a huge step from where he had been weeks earlier. Our family was grateful to be on our own again. We had needed our parents for so long. It was nice to feel some independence. God had brought us so far.

A couple days after having our home back, Jeremy and I needed to go somewhere. Stephen was at my parents, so we had Saturday to ourselves. Heaven knows how desperately we needed to reconnect after the months together but apart. I had sworn I would not drive for a very long time, if ever. The first time I rode in the front seat had been a big deal in itself. My Mom had taken me to Wal-Mart one afternoon, and I was shocked to realize how closely the windshield was to my face. Normal people would not even notice this, but I did. I kept my head down and eyes on the floorboard the whole time. Whenever I had rode in the van that transported us, my heart would stop with every punch of the brakes. It brought back so many memories. Needless to say, driving was not a top priority.

This particular Saturday, though, Jeremy and I had no other option. We didn't want to call anyone in our quest for independence. We wrote out II Timothy 1:7, " For the Spirit God gave us does not make us timid, but gives us power, love and self-discipline" and taped it to the car's dashboard. Jeremy prayed as I buckled the seatbelt. That day I healed, and each time after when I got behind the wheel I continued to heal. Our God is one of power not fear!

That same afternoon when we returned home, we decided to park in the garage as opposed to outside the front door. Doing this meant we would have to see the car we had wrecked. For insurance purposes, we had agreed to have the car stored in our garage until it could be moved. Jeremy and I parked the car I was driving and walked over to the vehicle that had almost taken our lives. We pulled back the tarp and through tears, began to inspect the mangled piece of metal. It was far worse than anything we had imagined. The pictures had not done it justice.

Jeremy and I held each other as we again realized what a miracle God had done. As we looked at the backseat where Stephen had been sitting we were overwhelmed. There was not a scratch back there. Jeremy could even open Stephen's door, much like David had done that night when he got him out. God had protected our son. Each day we remember how different things could have been. Each day we are thankful for God's present blessings.

That day we again healed. Many months later, as the car still sat in our garage, I would go down there, pull the tarp back, and weep. Some days I felt anger; others joy. On a couple occasions, I thought about grabbing the shovel from the wall and banging on the car to my heart's content. I would run my hand down the side of it and replay all that had happened that night. As glad as we were when the tow truck came to remove it, Jeremy and I are confident it was God's will that it be in our house. It helped us face what had happened and move on. I am thankful for those quiet moments in that garage.

Concerning how our church, Union Grove, stepped in on our behalf is an incredible thing. I could never truly explain it in the detail it deserves. To mention people's names would be a mistake. I would be sure to leave someone out. There were so many who helped.

Each day, from 9:00-11:00, a lady from the church would come over. She would watch Stephen while our families either showered or just rested a little. Some of them would bring him new toys and books. Often our Moms would find these willing women pushing Stephen in his stroller all the way up the large hill that is part of our driveway. This time was so important for our families. They were often beyond the point of exhaustion each morning when these ladies arrived.

Every other day, the MOPS group at our church would bring us lunch. Every night, someone from our church would deliver dinner. It would always be enough to feed us, the five or six members of our family who were always there, and probably the rest of our neighborhood! The food was always so good and catered to the things we liked. This was a big deal as Jeremy and I are very picky eaters. Often I would see people come in the front door who I knew had needs of their own. It was tremendous seeing their servants' hearts. They were loving us as God had loved them…wholeheartedly, no strings attached, asking nothing in return.

Once a week, someone from the church would come over and clean our house. They would do everything from sweeping to mopping to cleaning the toilets. A man from Union Grove would come over most Saturdays to mow our yard. Whenever we had an appointment, a van would be there to pick us up. Our Pastor's wife had set up a very effective system. We could not have made it through without these practical sacrifices.

The amount of cards we received was staggering. One afternoon there were 17 cards waiting for us in our mailbox. They came from all over the country and meant more to us than the writers will ever know. So many people brought us special gifts that we will treasure forever. From blankets to homemade rocking horses, we were often overwhelmed by others' thoughtfulness. One such time, someone came in with loads of groceries and completely stocked our pantry. Being a $20 a week grocery shopper back then, I was ecstatic. This was more food than we had ever had in our home!

When Jeremy and I found out that our yard was going to be landscaped, we were again flooded with tears of thankfulness. Coming home to our new front driveway had been amazing. We couldn't fathom anything more. As the landscape company arrived that morning, all eyes peeked out the kitchen window. Jeremy and I lay in our hospital beds and listened to the reports. From trees to bushes, truck after truck was arriving with shrubbery. No longer being able to handle the curiosity, Mom pushed my wheelchair to the window, so I could see myself. The images of all those trucks and those beautiful trees still lay fresh in my mind.

Later that afternoon the landscapers finished. They had been there all day. Our parents pushed both me and Jeremy outside, so we could see what had been done. I imagine both our mouths dropped open. It was absolutely beautiful! There were even red rose bushes! Jeremy was pleased to see they had even taken the time the dig up the few bushes we had recently planted and replanted them somewhere else.

As we sat in awe of our new yard, I asked Jeremy, "Is this really our yard?" Both of us kept saying that it was what we had always wanted. It was truly perfect.

Soon after the day the landscapers came, we were again surprised by someone's generosity. For years Jeremy and I had wanted to put up a decorative fence in our front yard. It would protect Stephen from falling off the retaining wall onto the concrete drive below. Financially, though, we could not do it. It was on our wish list.

This particular day, Jeremy and I sat and watched a man put up the fence we had always wanted (and needed). With each beautiful brown post, we saw another blessing. Not only did the fence match our house, it would protect Stephen in the future. Jeremy and I will forever be grateful to these servants who, without even knowing us, made some of the dreams for our home come true.

Since August 27, we have had the opportunity to meet many of the people on the wreck scene that evening. These are people we fondly call our heroes. The night we met David, who pulled Stephen out of the car, was heart-warming. He walked into our front door, and Jeremy immediately recognized him. I remembered his voice but not his face. David told us more details of how things were when he stopped at the scene. While we were talking,

Stephen came into the room. David stopped in mid-

sentence and began wiping away tears. He was

overwhelmed to see Stephen. We will forever be humbled

by David's willingness to help our family.

Suzanne and her family came over and visited us

one evening. I was excited to meet her husband, John, as he

was one of the few people I remembered from the wreck.

We sat and talked for awhile. Jeremy, for the first time, was

able to thank Suzanne for the CPR she did on Stephen.

I was able to thank John for talking me through those long

minutes in the car. He again told us what a miracle we

were. God had saved our lives that day. We could never

adequately share with this family how thankful we are to

them.

As time has passed, nearly 7 years have gone by.

The seemingly little things have become big deals to us. I

remember one night right after the wreck rubbing medicine

on Stephen's mosquito bites and wiping away the tears.

Most Moms would consider this duty but not me, not now.

For so many months I had been unable to hold or console

Stephen. I was grateful for the chance to help him in this

small way. Jeremy and I take nothing for granted: walking

is a big deal, taking a shower is so refreshing, doing the

laundry is a blessing. You never realize what you have until

it's taken or almost taken away. Time with family is so

important to us. We take special trips and plan surprise

outings. God has given us our lives back; we don't want to

miss or waste a moment.

Holidays that first year were more special than ever.

Christmas was so real. We did lots of little things to make

it memorable. On Christmas Eve we lit 10 luminaries we

had bought in support of the Ronald McDonald House. It

was beautiful and meant so much to us. Stephen's birthday

was also a huge thing. That day we took him to the zoo and

were grateful to walk around and show him all God's

beautiful creations. We had a Thomas party a couple days later. Our 6th wedding anniversary was very emotional. I flooded my pillow with tears as I again remembered how close we were to not having that special day.

On the one year anniversary of the wreck, our church was once again holding Revival services. That particular night they planned a dinner for those who impacted our lives during that time. The other driver and his family even came. It was so moving. During that week, Jeremy also received a call from the Summit Church in Durham. After much prayer, God led our family to that ministry. Jeremy is presently the Kids' Pastor and loves ministering to the families in our church. We believe that God was preparing him for that role through the wreck. He was opening his eyes to grace and the beauty of family. God has been and continues to be so faithful.

Yes, days slip by where we forget what happened; where we live our lives like before and fail to "turn up the music." Most of the time, however, we remember. And because we remember, things are seen and done differently. We spend time together. We never leave without saying I love you and giving a kiss. We avoid anger. We say thank You to the Father when a song or comment brings everything back. Life is so special; each day is truly a gift to be cherished. We want to "live life, not let it live us." We want God's love shown in the Gospel to be the constant source of peace in our lives. We want Him to be enough when life feels out of control. We want to love others as we have been loved. With God there is always hope. We don't ever want to forget what He's brought us through. We have been changed.

There are so many more stories woven around our Storm. As each year passes, we tend to discover something we didn't know before. We meet new people through random acquaintances who prayed for us. Only Heaven will allow us the chance to say thank you as we should.

And to think that in Heaven, we will finally be able to say

thank you to our Father. He, above any person, deserves the

praise. Yes, those months were hard. We know our future

has forever been changed. But more importantly, we know

that God is faithful. He doesn't change. His plan for August

27 was as perfect as His plans for every day of our lives.

Until we meet the Lord face to face, may we live with

hearts of gratefulness and seek to experience Him as

intimately as we have in recent days. He is life. To God be

the glory!

*All Scripture references are from the NKJV and NIV.

*Union Grove Baptist Church is located in Lexington, NC.

(ugbconline.com)

*The Summit Church is located in the Raleigh/Durham

area. (summitrdu.com)

*The majority of this book was written in 2007/2008 while

we recovered. The stories and details were so fresh. We

revised it a little in 2014 to update some personal

information. Since then our family has grown by 2 kids.

We were blessed by Esther Grace in 2014 and then

surprised by Kenan Samuel in 2015. Jeremy's job with the

Summit Church has also changed, and we are excited to see

how God uses him as Campus Pastor of the Alamance

Campus. The words of this book have become almost

nostalgic to us, so most of it sits untouched. The core of the

story will always stand. God is faithful. He was to our

parents Adam and Eve when He promised a Savior and He

continues to be today.

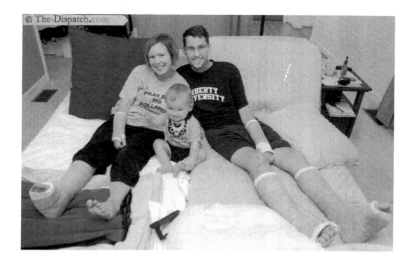

Made in the USA
Lexington, KY
27 October 2015